TEACHING THE NEW BASIC SKILLS

PRINCIPLES FOR EDUCATING CHILDREN TO THRIVE IN A CHANGING ECONOMY

RICHARD J. MURNANE
FRANK LEVY

MARTIN KESSLER BOOKS
THE FREE PRESS

For Patrick, Dan, and John,
who have enriched my life enormously, and most of all for
Mary Jo, a better friend one could not have.
RJM

For Floss, the memory of Ray, David, Marin,
and most of all for Kathy.
Teachers, every one of them.
FL

THE FREE PRESS
A Division of Simon & Schuster Inc.
1230 Avenue of the Americas
New York, NY 10020

Designed by Michael Mendelsohn of MM Design 2000, Inc.

Manufactured in the United States of America
10 9 8 7

Library of Congress Cataloging-in-Publication Data

Murnane, Richard J.
  Teaching the new basic skills: principles for educating children
to thrive in a changing economy/Richard J. Murnane, Frank Levy.
       p.   cm.
  Includes bibliographical references and index.
  ISBN 0–684–82739–5
  1. Basic education—United States. 2. Education—Economic
aspects—United States. 3. Career education—United States.
I. Levy, Frank. II. Title.
LC1035.6.M87   1996
370.11—dc20   96–13495
                                                        CIP

ISBN 0-684-82739-5

CONTENTS

FOREWORD

You are about to experience fresh and compelling arguments for education reform and learn about practical ways to manage schools to improve teaching and learning for all students. Academic economists Richard Murnane and Frank Levy bring us knowledge from their discipline and research to suggest practical ways to improve schools. Many educators are skeptical about academic economists being able to contribute much to the education reform debate: what could economists suggest about the management of schools for improved student results? "Schools are different from businesses. They have different purposes and customers." This is a limited view. In the past decade, school-business partnerships have become more common. Educators have been opening their doors to business people and accepting invitations to spend time in their places of work. Early experience with successful school-to-work programs demonstrates that the applied learning of the workplace can complement academic learning in the school and in the process motivate and engage students in learning without sacrificing academic standards. The corporate executive or manager of a local business who serves as principal for a day in a public school both teaches and learns, as does the teacher or principal who spends time with a business mentor.

A great deal of skepticism remains as educators and business people become more willing to learn from each other. Murnane and Levy take on the skeptics with a sensible explanation of practices used in successful businesses that could help improve schools. They are not uncritical of business, which they acknowledge makes mistakes, but they remind us of the obvious—successful businesses learn from their mistakes and do not repeat them. Moreover, successful businesses are very savvy about the context in which they operate and quick to notice how it is changing. Schools should be too.

Recently I spent two fascinating hours in the auditorium of Boston English High School watching teams from two Boston middle schools, the Lewenberg and the Timilty, compete for the citywide Academic League championship. There were several rounds to the competition. Some were structured with the spotlight on individual team members as they attempted to answer questions about geography, history, mathematics, science, language usage, and other challenging subjects while seconds ticked away on the electronic scoreboard clock. In another round, a group from each team was sent to a separate room to prepare a team response to the question: how would you evaluate President Clinton's first term?

The teams had been forewarned a week earlier that the question would focus on the Clinton presidency, but they did not receive the specific question until the beginning of the championship match. While their teammates handled the questions in rounds one and two, the problem-solving groups were developing their team presentations for the judges. When round three began, each team had five minutes to make its case for the judges and every team member had a role in the presentation. The last round was a fast-paced free-for-all where the team member hitting the buzzer first got to answer the question. The stakes were high—a correct answer gave the team one point, but a wrong answer resulted in a one-point deduction. The final score was the Timilty Middle School 55 and the Lewenberg Middle School 54. The Timilty retained its citywide championship for a second year.

What these students were demonstrating by their performance was nothing new for those whose reference point is the select group of students who assume they will continue their post-secondary education at four-year colleges and universities. But something was different. These students represented a cross-section of a demographically diverse urban school district where educators, parents, students, and the community are beginning to recognize that all students must leave high school today with the knowledge and ability to apply what we once required of only the select few who continued their formal education in colleges and universities. As recently as the 1950s, twenty percent of the jobs in America were professional, twenty percent skilled and sixty percent unskilled. In the 1990s, the percentage of professional jobs is about the same, but skilled jobs have soared to sixty-plus percent while unskilled jobs have fallen below twenty percent. Communities are beginning to recognize that the demands of the labor market are changing. Schools like the Lewenberg and the Timilty have begun to deal with these changes productively.

No longer will today's high school diploma lead to a job that will provide a wage that will guarantee entry to the middle class. The entire economy has changed dramatically and will continue to do so. A recent report by the Massachusetts Institute for Social and Economic Research projected that there will be 385,000 jobs created in Massachusetts by the year 2010. They will demand skills that do not exist in the current Massachusetts workforce. Some may take solace in early 1996 that the economic indicators are strong and that the economic imperative should not be so pervasive in the debate about the goals of education. The recession seems to be over and America once again appears to be the most competitive among the economic superpowers in the global economy. Trend data are less convincing. This is my view of the context Richard Murnane and Frank Levy explain to shape our understanding of what skills students will need to be successful and how schools must be managed to ensure students are educated for the changing economy.

It may be a tough sell for the American public. Early in 1996, many polls find public education to be at the top of the public's list of concerns. Many of the specific concerns are not new: safety, discipline, achievement, student drug use, to name a few, are issues that have been central to schools for a long time. While confidence in the schools located close to where one lives remains relatively high, particularly among parents of children attending those schools, confidence in schools in general has fallen. When asked to describe what should be done to improve the schools, some consensus emerges, but there is still a good deal of ambivalence about what to continue and what to change. Many adults presume that if schools were more like the ones they remember attending, they would improve significantly. A reality check is necessary, and the authors help us make it. The sentiment about returning to the good old days may be changing as people losing their jobs when corporations "rightsize" find that they do not have the required skills to move to the new jobs now available in a changing economy This may reflect what Secretary of Labor Robert Reich recently meant when he said there are three classes of people in America—poor, rich and anxious.

I like the "five principles for educating children in a changing economy" identified by Murnane and Levy as they looked at several of America's most successful companies and improving schools. They provide a practical way for educators to think about managing schools to prepare students for the changing economy. This is not a book about the declining educational quality of our schools, but rather an acknowledgment that the economy is changing faster than the schools and that, with good management, the schools can respond and serve students well.

What is the evidence that the schools have not kept pace with what the economy requires? The authors present persuasive data. What a high school graduate has to offer most employers is no longer in demand. The gap between the average annual earning of high school and college graduates has widened significantly in the past fifteen years. Employers are paying more for skills college graduates bring to the workplace, which enables these employees to earn a middle class income. The authors believe that college will not be a prerequisite for earning a middle-class income in the future if high school graduates possess the New Basic Skills. They describe them as the "hard skills" of basic mathematics, problem solving, and reading at higher levels and the "soft skills" of working effectively in groups, making effective oral and written presentations, and using computers well. From best business practice, the authors found that skilled employees and good management produce outstanding results. Their studies of schools demonstrate that the management principles used by the firms also can work in schools.

Each of the five principles common to management in business and schools could provide the starting point for school improvement, but when applied interdependently, they can have a dramatic impact. Educators attempting systemic reform will understand. Ensuring frontline workers' understanding of the problems to be addressed is the first principle. Schools do have some challenges business can avoid because students and parents, as well as educators, are frontline workers. The second principle, providing clear incentives and opportunities to participate in solutions, is easier for business than for schools because the non-employees (parents and students) may not respond to the same incentives as employees. For example, the authors cite compelling research showing that too many American parents and students believe innate ability is more important than effort in determining student achievement. High-quality employee training is the third principle. Fourth is regular measurement of progress. The fifth principle is perseverance and learning from mistakes.

The principles make good sense. Murnane and Levy explain why the five principles do not more easily shape good management practices in schools. Educators do not know the skills employers now require of the people they hire. Business does not require evidence of performance in school as a condition of employment and therefore students have few incentives to work hard. Training for educators often is unconnected to the purpose of the school and presented in stand-alone programs without follow-up that provides teachers with insights on how to improve instruction in the classroom. Tests may not measure what is taught. And the search for simple solutions to complex problems continues, although most educators really know that there are no quick fixes.

Most educational reformers do not write about the management of schools. Questions of incentives, job design, methods of measuring progress, obtaining agreement on goals, while at the core of most discussions of improving the performance of firms, rarely are included in discussions of how to improve schools. The authors argue that they should be and demonstrate that they can be central to a comprehensive strategy for school improvement.

Readers with any doubts about the understanding that Murnane and Levy have about what takes place in schools should take extra time with Chapter 6 on professional development. It resonates with educators' descriptions of what professional development activities typically look like and what it will take to make such activities connect content and pedagogy, meet standards of high quality, and become sustained strategies for improving teaching in the school.

It is important to underscore the interdependence of the five management principles particularly for schools. Too many efforts to improve schools have been fragmented and piecemeal. In an attempt to try a little bit of everything, schools continue to add new projects and programs while rarely letting anything go. In the best cases, progress is measured for an individual project, but the impact on teaching and learning schoolwide is ignored. Little is pursued in depth. There are too many demands on the curriculum. Educators, parents, and students fail to grasp that some things are more important to teach and learn than others. Improved teaching and learning for all students should be the shared goal. Use of the five management principles can help bring educators and parents together as they develop a comprehensive schoolwide plan which connects high expectations for students, curriculum, instructional practice, training, assessment, school governance, accountability, parent involvement, and partnerships with the overall purposes of teaching and learning. The whole plan for improvement becomes greater than the sum of its parts.

I am a strong proponent of setting high expectations and standards for what students should learn. I believe in providing more choice for parents within the public school system. I know that more resources are necessary to enable the schools to meet the needs of students once met by other institutions in the society. And I realize that advocacy for more resources begins with producing convincing evidence about how current resources are being used to raise student skills. The authors' cautions about embracing some of these reform strategies are compelling. What is important is how they help guide schools toward comprehensive changes that result in improved teaching and learning. The examples of the schools that effectively embraced the five principles offer encouragement for all of us who understand the urgency of improving our schools now.

I began my career in education as a history and government teacher and believe now as I did then that it is not good enough to have only the economic engine in front pulling the education train to the workplace. Other engines must be pulling to equally important destinations. We worry about the strength of our economy, but must not take for granted the vibrancy of our democracy. Our vigilance in educating for responsible citizenship should not be diminished by our understanding of economic realities.

There is no question that we must develop new economic capital, but we also must find ways to create new social capital. Our young people must connect to both to become productive workers and responsible citizens. Use of the five management principles can help schools improve what they do to enable all students to become responsible adults who will keep the economy strong and the democracy vibrant. What is at stake is the quality of life for everyone.

Thomas W. Payzant
Superintendent
Boston Public Schools

FOREWORD

Richard Murnane and Frank Levy's *Teaching the New Basic Skills* confronts one of the most pressing social issues of our day—the increasingly dramatic disparity between the skills children are currently acquiring within our educational system and the skills they will need to obtain good jobs in an increasingly selective, globally influenced job market. As Murnane and Levy point out in this useful and important book, the skills required to earn a decent income have changed radically, but what is taught in most of our schools has changed little, if at all. Motorola is a corporation which has been undergoing the same dramatic changes as those excellent companies the authors use as models in *Teaching the New Basic Skills*. During the past fifteen years, the strategy of Motorola has moved from a focus on building the best hardware and software in the world to one based on the realization that it is "world class mindware" which determines the competitiveness of Motorola. Our strategy is now driven by the process of recruiting, selecting, hiring, and retaining world class people so that we will have products and services which exceed our customer's expectations. In this process we have discovered that, just as the statistics in *Teaching the New Basic Skills* warn, we can only hire 10 percent of the entry-level candidates who apply for employment in our United States operations. This dismal statistic has forced us to examine the situation with our "supply base" for human resources, the education system. The question that this book presents, and that we must all answer is, "Is the pre-kindergarten through university system in this country developing students who have the skills necessary to be successful in a workplace driven by continuous change in a global, competitive environment?" The data in this book, as well as what we have experienced ourselves, indicate that the answer to this question is no. Murnane and Levy point out that there are examples in the education system of "heroes doing heroic things," which prepare some children for a successful life after their formal education ends. In general, there are improvements being made in the curriculum, instruction, and assessment methods utilized in schools. The major issue, however, is that the education system is undergoing *incremental improvement* in an environment of *exponential change*. This fact implies that educational improvement at the present rate will result in fewer and fewer young people being prepared for a global economy. If we together, business people and educators, allow this to happen, the future of our country is in doubt.

Teaching the New Basic Skills poses serious and difficult questions that all of us will have to consider. Since Motorola has struggled for the past fifteen years in this changing world and managed not only to survive, but also to take on world class status, what have we learned that might be transferable to the education system? Can we add anything to the five principles Murnane and Levy describe in this book that will assist the reader in applying those principles to his or her own situation? As the book's fifth principle states, "there are no magic bullets." But there are some concepts and processes that may assist in accelerating the changes that must occur in the system responsible for educating our young.

A basic premise for our discussion is that the system cannot be "reformed." You cannot reshape what presently exists because the model is obsolete. Just as when Motorola set goals of a 100-fold improvement in the quality of our products and services and found that conventional wisdom would never allow us to achieve those goals, unconventional thinking is now necessary to achieve the necessary transformation in the education system. We use the word "transform" to indicate that education must utilize a new model of teaching and learning. Motorola is continuously transforming itself through internal renewal. Educators must now follow a similar path.

As *Teaching the New Basic Skills* emphasizes, leadership is a crucial factor in any such transformation. Leaders must have the courage to take risks and believe in the abilities of the people in their organizations. The role of the leader is to set very high expectations for the organization (e.g., Motorola's goal of improving the quality of everything we do by 100 percent) and then to put in place the support systems that enable every person in the organization to work together to achieve the goal collectively. As Murnane and Levy point out, leaders must establish an environment in which workers feel respected and valued. The training is the primary way to accelerate change as people learn to use new processes and tools in their work. The transformation in education *cannot* be accomplished without investing in the development of teachers and administrators. School principals and superintendents need as much training and development as teachers, only in different areas of expertise. Investment in the training of what this book calls the "frontline worker" is only useful if a prior investment has been made in those responsible for the leadership and management of the frontline worker.

We cannot emphasize this last point enough. Improvements in organizations cannot occur without leaders who develop an environment of trust so that every employee is willing to take the risks associated with change in that organization. Education system leaders, including superintendents, principals, school boards, and union members, are all vital participants in the process of transformation. They must take responsibility for investing in themselves and each other to ensure that each has the knowledge and skills necessary to lead systematic change.

Since change in all systems, private and public, is accelerating at such a rapid pace, the continuous learning recommended in *Teaching the New Basic Skills* is absolutely necessary. For us here at Motorola, the most critical skill required by the workforce is just such an ability to learn and keep learning. While most descriptions of necessary skills for children do not list "learning to learn," this should be the capstone skill upon which all others depend. Memorized facts, which are the basis for most testing done in schools today, are of little use in the age in which information is doubling every two or three years. We have expert systems in computers and the Internet that can provide the facts we need when we need them. Our workforce needs to utilize facts to assist in developing solutions to problems. The worker needs to be able to utilize the systems which give him or her "just-in-time" access to information when it's required in the problem-solving process.

In our view, the mission of the education system has three components: to develop socially responsible, employable young people with lifelong learning skills. This mission cannot be achieved without the collaboration of the community in the development of social responsibility and the business sector in the definition of employability.

The role of community is often understated in terms of a necessary involvement in the transformation of learning systems for children. In our corporation, we use the statistic that children attend school only 9 percent of the time they are alive from birth to age 18. It is what happens to children in the 91 percent of the time (the "91 percent factor") that has a much greater impact on children's success in life than what happens in the 9 percent of the time in school. We cannot expect even a transformed education system to overcome the influence of the 91 percent factor. Therefore, we all have responsibilities for the development of socially responsible youth. The often-used old African proverb that "It takes the entire village to raise a child" is even more true today.

The business sector has a major role in the development of the "employability" component of the mission of the education system. We in industry must clearly articulate what skills are required for a student to be employable. Much work has been done in this area by the SCANS commission (Secretary's Commission on Achieving Necessary Skills) and the present National Skills Standards Board (NSSB). But it is not enough for the business community to list the criteria for work. We must take an active role in translating our definitions into processes which have meaning and application in the classroom. We must assist teachers in understanding how work is done so they can create a relevancy to the subjects children are learning. We need to assist teachers in answering a student's question "why do I need to learn algebra?" Business and education must work together collaboratively to share resources and experience and collectively develop a system preparing young people to do productive work.

The education system has the major responsibility for developing a young person who has "learned to learn." This must begin with the integration of recent research on learning into the curriculum of the colleges of education. Teachers must model collaboration in the classroom. The system must be sensitive to the individual learning styles of every child. Since the workplace is now driven by problem solving teams, children must learn to work together cooperatively in developing multiple solutions to real-world situations. The system must do away with existing time constraints (50-minute periods, 180-day school years) because young people don't all learn at the same rate. The education system must adapt to meet the needs of the child rather than forcing the child to meet the needs of the system.

As we have stated and as this book describes, none of what is required will come easily. The continuous improvement process in Motorola has taken 15 years and has been a painful process, throughout which many mistakes have been made. But we have learned from those mistakes and through our learning created a higher social good for our employees, suppliers, and customers throughout the world. But this process cannot continue without an education system which is preparing young people to be successful in the world which is changing every day. We must begin this journey together.

Robert W. Galvin
Chairman of the Executive Committee
Motorola

Edward W. Bales
Director of Education–External Systems
Motorola

ACKNOWLEDGMENTS

This book is about people working to improve the schools and firms in which they work. It could only have been written with the support of a great many persons. They include James Ehrenstrom and John Kordsmeier of Northwestern Mutual Life; Don English and Dennis Lee of Honda of America; Christine Ziehman of Diamond-Star Motors (now Mitsubishi Motors of America); Mary Tenopyr of AT&T; Craig Perry of the Industrial Metal Products Company; Al Ondis of AstroMed, Inc.; staff members at Martin-Marietta, and Aetna Insurance; Ernesto Cortes, Joe Higgs, and Kathleen Davis of the Texas Industrial Areas Foundation; Alejandro Mindiz-Melton and the teachers and parents of Zavala Elementary School in East Austin, Texas; the teachers and students at Hope High School in Providence, Rhode Island, and at Bethesda–Chevy Chase High School in Bethesda, Maryland; Lois Ann Porter and Phillisa Prescott of the Boston Private Industry Council; the teachers and students of Boston ProTech—especially Pam McDonall and Tony Barbosa; Rick Mills, Jill Rosenblum, Sue Rigney, and a great many Vermont teachers. In addition, we would like to thank the management of Sports Plus and the administration and fifth-grade teachers of the Cabot public schools for their help. The Cabot schools and Sports Plus are the only two organizations identified by pseudonyms in the book.

Patricia Graham, Richard Nelson, and Edward Pauly read an early draft of the entire manuscript and provided many ideas for improvements. Harold Howe and Charles Abelmann provided helpful comments on drafts of several chapters. We would like to thank the great many colleagues who gave us helpful feedback on individual chapters.

Barbara Ankeny, an editor and a friend, helped us at the very beginning though she and we knew she would not live to see the book completed. Our agent, Helen Rees, kept us focused on a book someone might want to read. Martin Kessler of The Free Press signed us on and provided encouragement before his untimely death. In finishing the book, we had the benefit of real enthusiasm and good ideas from Susan Arellano, our editor at The Free Press. Ann Hawthorne, an editor in Cambridge, substantially improved the prose of a next-to-last draft.

A grant from the Spencer Foundation made it possible for us to undertake a project of this scope. The Russell Sage Foundation, the Sloan Foundation, and the Daniel Rose Chair in Economics at MIT provided additional support. We owe them all our thanks.

We would like to thank our children, John and Dan Murnane, David and Marin Levy, for tolerating our ups, downs, and our many trips to learn about schools and firms struggling to change. Special thanks go to our wives, Mary Jo Murnane and Katherine Swartz, who supported us with goodwill while coping with the stresses of their own careers. To all of them we say thanks for sticking with us.

CHAPTER 1

PREPARING TO MEET THE FUTURE

East Austin, Texas. Zavala Elementary School is a two-story yellow-brick structure built in 1936 and now connected by walkways to 18 portable classrooms. The school sits on tree-lined Robert Martinez Jr. Street between Santa Rita Courts and Chalmers Courts, two Hispanic public housing projects.

T. A. Vasquez lives around the corner from Zavala Elementary. All four of her children went to school there. Her third child, Cynthia, had a solid B average in first-grade math, and T. A. assumed Cynthia was doing well. Nobody at Zavala Elementary told T. A. that Cynthia and most of her classmates were scoring at the fifteenth percentile on the Texas statewide mathematics test. The problem was real but things would get better.

Cabot, Massachusetts. Audubon Elementary School is a long way from Zavala Elementary both in terms of miles (about 1,900) and in terms of money. The average Zavala family makes about $12,000 per year; the average Audubon family makes $90,000. Still, Audubon Elementary had its problems.

Sharon Wright was picking her way through broken light

bulbs on the floor of her fifth-grade classroom. Earlier in the year, Sharon and seven other Cabot fifth-grade teachers took a 10-week afterschool course designed just for them. The teachers thought they would learn to lead fifth-graders in hands-on experiments on the physics of light. Instead, they got two-hour lectures on theory that kept them prisoners in their chairs. They had no chance to try the experiments they were eventually supposed to lead. Now as Sharon walked among her class of 23, with extension cords crisscrossing the floor, she winced as yet another light bulb broke. The problems were real but things would get better.

This book is about the skills students now need to succeed in the economy and how schools can change to teach those skills. We begin by visiting a set of U.S. factories and offices—two automobile factories, an insurance company, a sporting-goods wholesaler. We will see the skills required of employees and the management principles under which they work. In most of these firms, skilled employees and good management go hand in hand: a skilled person assigned to a dumb job will produce little and earn less.

Then we will visit a set of places where people are learning how to teach the skills good employers require—poor schools, rich schools, a hospital pathology laboratory, a teachers' summer "camp" in Vermont. In these places, teachers like Sharon Wright and parents like T. A. Vasquez are doing the dirty work of school improvement: building a constituency for higher standards, constructing better incentives for students, moving teacher training beyond one-day workshops, creating tests that measure what students need to learn. Much of their work also involves management principles. To raise student skills, T. A. Vasquez, Sharon Wright, and others we will meet are making an effort comparable to reengineering a midsize business. An important part of America's future depends on how well they succeed.

THE COST OF COMPETITIVENESS

During the past 20 years, the skills required to succeed in the economy have changed radically, but the skills taught in most schools have changed very little. As a result of the ever-growing mismatch between the skills of most graduates and the skills required by high-wage employers, a U.S. high school diploma is no longer a ticket to the U.S. middle class.

As late as 1979, a 30-year-old man with a U.S. high school diploma earned a yearly average of $27,700, in 1993 dollars. That income, combined with a wife's earnings from a part-time job, secured the family a solid place in the middle class. Then, almost without warning, the economy changed. By 1983 U.S. manufacturing, threatened by imports, was rapidly downsizing, and a 30-year-old man with a high school diploma earned an average of $23,000 a year, in 1993 dollars. By 1993, with computers transforming both U.S. manufacturing and U.S. services, a 30-year-old man with a high school diploma earned an average of $20,000. The significance of this decline in earnings becomes all the greater when we realize that in 1993 *half* of all 30-year-old men had not gone beyond high school.

By the early 1990s, the need for a quality education extended beyond high school graduates. At all levels, the economy was forcing people to become economic free agents, constantly prepared to prove their worth in the market. Today's firms increasingly set pay based on an employee's recent performance, not long-term relationships. Jobs at IBM and AT&T now end abruptly and people must resell themselves. In this world you go to war every day, and short of being a millionaire, a very good education is your best armor.

Viewed from a distance, the economy's changes represent progress, the rebuilding of the nation's economic efficiency. In both 1994 and 1995, the United States was rated the most competitive economy in the world, a ranking unthinkable a decade earlier.[1]

But rebuilding efficiency has exacted big human costs. The costs are clearest among men and women who have not gone beyond high school, but uncertainty now affects men and women at every level. The issue is not that U.S. educational quality has declined—standardized test scores are modestly higher today than in the early 1980s.[2] But the economy is changing much faster than the schools have improved. Many people—including roughly half of recent graduates—have an education that is no longer in demand.

The nation cannot absorb change of this magnitude without political consequences. The consequences began in the 1994 elections when all aspects of competitiveness were on display. In aggregate terms, the economy was booming: unemployment had fallen below 5.5 percent; inflation was a low 2.7 percent; labor productivity, the ultimate measure of the economy's efficiency, was growing faster than in the two previous decades. But the wages of high school graduates— younger and older, men and women—did not increase. And some men and women with college diplomas found their jobs eliminated through downsizing. For many voters, hope turned to anger, and the elections offered a variety of targets for blame: the president, Congress, welfare mothers, affirmative action, multinational corporations.

Missing from this list was a growing determinant of

incomes—the quality of U.S. schools. Schools were not a high-priority issue, not even among voters with school-age children. The reason why begins in public opinion polls.

In the case of schools, American public opinion is best described as schizophrenic. When Americans are asked about schools in general, the verdict is negative. In 1995, only 20 percent of Americans rated the nation's public schools as A or B, down from 27 percent in 1986. But when American *parents with children in public schools* are asked about *their children's* schools, the picture is much brighter. In 1995, 65 percent of parents gave a rating of A or B to the school attended by their oldest child, a figure as high as in 1986. When pressed to name a problem in their local public schools, 11 percent of public school parents cited poor discipline and 8 percent cited violence. Only 4 percent faulted educational quality.[3]

Parental satisfaction is important because when parents are *dis*satisfied with their children's schools, the politicians notice and the schools can change. In the last 15 years, parents of handicapped children have pushed to get their children moved into regular classes, and schools have responded. Large numbers of parents have pushed schools to teach about drug abuse, smoking, and, in some cases, AIDS; and the schools have responded. Compared to these issues, higher student skills attracted little parental interest. From a political perspective, there was not much to debate.[4]

Why didn't parents press for more rigorous skills? It isn't that parents don't care. Among adults who rated their local schools as better than the average public school, 79 percent cited the local school's greater emphasis on high academic achievement as the primary reason.[5] But parents have read that test scores are slowly rising. They see their children learning as much in school and doing as much homework as they did. They see that the schools are teaching their children at least as many skills as they, themselves, learned in school.

But until quite recently, many parents *did not* see that the skills that were sufficient to earn a good living in 1970 are not good enough today. Changes in the economy have made the standard U.S. high school education a glut on the market. These same changes require a sounder education at all levels of schooling.

Now, under the constant pounding of the economy, parental attitudes have begun to change. In the most recent Gallup poll, the percentage of adults supporting higher standards for promotion stood at 87 percent, up from 70 percent in 1979.[6] Similarly, a 1995 poll by the Public Agenda Foundation probed parental attitudes and found beneath the surface satisfaction a growing worry that their children's education was inadequate. In this poll, 41 percent of parents with children in public schools said that a high school diploma is not a guarantee that a student has learned the basics. The results also showed strong support for a greater emphasis on basic skills and on standards for promotion and graduation.[7] In this book, we show how teachers and parents are translating this amorphous discontent into better schools.

WHERE WILL ALL THE SMART KIDS WORK?

Suppose the increasing obsolescence of the education provided by most U.S. schools is allowed to continue. What will happen? The outcome is not hard to imagine. The children of the wealthy and clever will be clustered in privileged schools—public and private—that do emphasize appropriate skills. These children will get good education and the good jobs, and the vast majority of other children will compete for what is left.

Despite this future, some persons argue that better schools are a dead end. The economy, they say, produces only a certain number of good jobs, so educating too many people too well will only drive down the wages of skilled workers. This argument has a surface plausibility. And its logic is correct *in the short run*. Train more people to be physicians, and in the short run, the wages of physicians will fall. But in the long run, rising productivity raises the wages of any worker who is in demand. In 1950, the United States had one physician for every 653 people. By 1990, there was one physician for every 406 people. And yet over this time, physicians' average incomes grew from $75,000 to $180,000 (in 1993 dollars),[8] a faster growth than occurred in the earnings of most other occupations. Over four decades, physicians could both increase their supply and increase their paychecks because they were an occupation in demand.

But suppose physicians had not been in demand. Suppose they had been like the farm laborers of 1949 whose jobs were being eliminated every day by new tractors and threshers. Faced with technical obsolescence, farm laborers had two alternatives: find a new line of work, or remain a farm laborer at ever lower wages, no matter how the economy was growing.

Many farm laborers found new work by moving to cities and taking manufacturing jobs. They could make the move because they already had the skills required for the jobs the city could offer. The corresponding move today—from displaced factory worker to customer service representative—is much harder because the customer service representative's job requires skills that many factory workers don't have.

The displaced factory worker's situation highlights the real effect of keeping education weak: the exclusion of many students from the high-skilled sectors of the economy, the sectors that by all projections will be growing and able to sustain high wages over the decades to come.

COLLEGE FOR EVERYONE?

In the chapters that follow, we emphasize improvements in K–12 education, and this raises a final objection. Isn't it true, one might ask, that a student has to go to college to be middle class today? After all, the earnings of college graduates have held up quite well over the last 15 years even as the earnings of high school graduates have declined.

If four (expensive) years of college were required to enter the middle class, it would pose an enormous obstacle to mobility. Fortunately, the apparent importance of college depends as much on what K–12 schools are *not* doing as on what is learned in college. In Chapter 2 we show that the widening earnings gap between high school and college graduates stems in large part from differences in the mastery of basic skills *when the two groups were high school seniors.* In other words, as high-wage employers increasingly search for new workers with strong basic skills they tend to bypass high school graduates who did not go to college, because so many of them lack those skills. Hiring college graduates solves the problem of finding workers with stronger basic skills, but college is a very expensive employment agency. If all students left high school with strong basic skills, the picture would be much different.

TEACHING THE NEW BASIC SKILLS

The challenge facing Sharon Wright and T. A. Vasquez begins with two questions:

- What are the New Basic Skills—the skills needed today to earn a middle-class income?
- What are the principles around which a school can restructure to teach these skills to all children?

The answer to the first question comes from our review of U.S. businesses in Chapters 2 and 3. Along with the characteristics that employers have always sought in new workers—reliability, a positive attitude, and a willingness to work hard—the employee-recruiting and work practices in firms paying high wages show the growing importance of a new set of skills:

- The hard skills: basic mathematics, problem-solving and reading abilities at levels much higher than many high school graduates now attain
- The "soft" skills: the ability to work in groups and to make effective oral and written presentations—skills many schools do not teach
- The ability to use personal computers to carry out simple tasks like word processing

These are the New Basic Skills needed by all students,

whether they go on to college or not, regardless of gender, regardless of race.

The answer to the second question comes from our visits to teaching sites in Chapters 4 through 7. In unexpected ways, the management principles emerging at these sites look very much like the management principles firms now use to manage skilled workers. Comparing selected schools and firms shows why this is no coincidence.

LEARNING THE RIGHT LESSON FROM BUSINESS

Many analysts argue that schools can learn from business because competition forces business "to get it right." In the chapters that follow we will see that, to the contrary, schools can learn from business because business often gets it wrong—but the best of business has learned to recover from mistakes in new and important ways.

In economics textbooks, a business is always looking for new opportunities, nimbly moving from success to success. A real-world business is much more erratic, cycling between periods of great success and periods of ineptitude. More precisely, the great success often *causes* the ineptitude.

Consider Ford Motor Company early in the century. By 1916, Henry Ford's Model T had become a triumph. It was the first car built on a modern assembly line and so could be sold at a low price. By 1921 it accounted for more than half of all cars sold in the nation. But success caused Ford Motor Company to turn inward. The market changed. Other companies developed more stylish and more powerful cars. Ford Motor Company kept making Model T's with only small improvements, trying to repeat past triumphs exactly. By

1926, Ford Motor was in crisis, its dealers in revolt, its market share below 30 percent and falling fast.[9]

Consider the more recent experience of the Wang Corporation of Lowell, Massachusetts. In 1981 Wang dominated the emerging market for word processors. Wang's systems were cumbersome—terminals connected by cables to bulky, single-purpose minicomputers. But they offered the miracle of an electronic document that could be easily changed. The word processor brought Wang enormous success, and Wang brought Lowell a level of prosperity not seen since the nineteenth-century heyday of the city's textile mills. Then success caused Wang to turn inward. The market changed. Apple and IBM developed small, flexible personal computers. Software programs like WordStar and WordPerfect allowed a user to do word processing on those computers. Wang continued to produce single-purpose minicomputers—the configuration that had brought it success. In 1991 the Wang Corporation declared bankruptcy, later reemerging as a much smaller, software-only firm.

In the 1960s and 1970s, U.S. schools were like Ford in 1916 and Wang in 1981. Most high school graduates were in the middle class. Parents and employers agreed that the schools were doing their job.[10] But success caused schools to turn inward. At the end of the 1970s, schools rarely talked to employers or parents about skills, because high school graduates were still faring relatively well in the labor market. In the 1980s, that market began to change rapidly. With the advent of more technology and more international trade, high school graduates were suddenly scrambling for a decent wage and college graduates were looking for new jobs. But this was something that happened to people *after* they graduated. Most schools, focused inward, missed the changes.

How do organizations regain success? Until the 1980s, the process of business recovery offered little that was helpful to schools. Most recoveries involved creating a new product with the old processes—Ford's Model A replacing the Model T. But in the past decade, demands for higher-quality goods and services have forced firms to recover by developing both new products *and new processes*. In modern manufacturing plants, employees use statistical process control to monitor quality and to diagnose problems. In a modern insurance company, a customer service representative armed with computer technology answers most questions directly instead of telling the customer to call a different department or to wait on hold for 10 minutes.

These new processes improve organizational performance through heavy reliance on the skills and initiative of front-line workers. To tap these skills and initiative, management has learned to design work according to new principles.

Go back to Ford Motor Company in 1916. In the River Rouge plant, each production worker had a very narrow job—say, installing the left front wheel on a Model T. That's all he was supposed to do. Because the job was narrow, it was easy for the supervisor to assess worker performance by answering simple questions: Was the worker keeping up with the assembly line? Was the wheel securely attached?

Now move forward to today's Honda of America plant in Marysville, Ohio. The person who installs the wheel here must also monitor the quality of the installation, move over to help other employees when they have trouble, work in groups to solve production problems, and constantly suggest ways to improve assembly line performance. Through this organization, Honda and other automobile manufacturers are able to continuously raise quality and lower cost—something that was much harder in Henry Ford's day.

But in the Honda plant today, a supervisor finds it much harder to rate workers than did a supervisor in a traditional Ford plant. Many of the most important activities are now products of group interactions, not of repetitive actions by individuals. The group activities depend on taking initiative and applying skills. Suppose one of the bolts holding the left front wheel is misaligned on every car, and a group of workers, formed to solve the problem, has not yet found the solution. Is it because the workers are thinking hard and the problem is subtle? Or is it because the workers are thinking about the Chicago Bulls?

Without entering a worker's mind, the supervisor can't answer these questions. That is the central truth of the new processes. Because initiative and the application of skills are not easily measured, supervisors cannot use the threat of frequent checks to guarantee worker performance. Rather, they have to rely on employee initiative and knowledge, and they have to think very hard about how those qualities can be fostered.

A school that would teach the New Basic Skills faces a similar management problem. It must help teachers to learn to teach the new material. It must devise different kinds of tests that better assess what students actually understand. It must raise expectations among teachers, students, and parents about what a young person needs to know today to enter the middle class. It must find ways to engage students' attention and energy.

Like the work at Honda, managing these processes is very subtle. It can't be checked by simply counting the hours spent by students in algebra or by teachers in professional development workshops. As at Honda, success depends on the initiative and skills of all the participants—teachers, parents, and students. And so here, too, management must think very hard about how these qualities can be fostered.

How do managers foster initiative and skill? The details differ across organizations. But best-practice firms that succeed in continually improving their product embrace five common principles:

1. Ensure that all frontline workers understand the problem.
2. Design jobs so that all frontline workers have both incentives and opportunities to contribute to solutions.
3. Provide all frontline workers with the training needed to pursue solutions effectively.
4. Measure progress on a regular basis.
5. Persevere and learn from mistakes; there are no magic bullets.

In Chapter 3 we show how best-practice firms have developed and implemented these principles, using them as a package. They realize that implementing only one or two of the five principles is not enough—providing good incentives to untrained workers won't get the job done.

In reorganizing to teach the New Basic Skills, the schools we describe in Chapters 4 through 7 are using the same principles adapted to reflect the ways in which schools differ from firms. Consider the differences between frontline workers at Honda of America and at East Austin's Zavala Elementary School. Honda's organization chart shows production associates in assembly, painting, welding, parts stamping, and engine production. Honda's success depends on giving these associates the skills and incentives to advance Honda's goals.

Identifying and managing the frontline workers at Zavala Elementary School is more of a challenge. Certainly its teachers, like Honda's production associates, are frontline workers paid to contribute to the organization. And as at Honda, providing teachers with skills and incentives to improve Zavala's performance is a big part of restructuring. But at Zavala, the students and their parents also qualify as frontline workers; their actions, too, are central to the learning process. Since students and parents aren't paid school employees, providing them with the right incentives is much more difficult, but it remains critical.

Take students first. We will show in Chapter 2 that mastery of basic mathematics has a bigger impact on the earnings of 24-year-old high school graduates today than in the late 1970s.[11] So skills pay off eventually, and the return is greater than in the past. But even today, mathematics mastery has no impact on a 20-year-old's earnings. The reason is simple. Because schools and employers rarely talk, employers have little idea which recent graduates have the New Basic Skills, and so performance in school has little impact on a graduate's first job. The immediate message to students is that skills don't matter. So why do the hard work to master these skills?

Many parents, especially those whose education did not extend beyond high school, have similar attitudes. Because they fail to see the close connection between the New Basic Skills and earnings, they see little reason to insist that their children turn off the TV and work hard on homework every night. As long as students and parents see the world in this way, rigorous education is not a reasonable goal.

In adapting the Five Principles, schools also understand that they lack certain options available to business. Engaging teachers, parents, and children at Zavala Elementary is hard work. If Zavala were a business, the school principal would have been tempted to change his suppliers—to recruit better-educated and more affluent families, as Honda could do with a supplier that was consistently sending faulty parts. If Zavala could recruit more affluent families, the test scores of children there would almost certainly rise (although test scores would fall in the schools that took the students Zavala had rejected). But, of course, recruiting families is not something Zavala can do. Like most U.S. public schools, it is required by its state's constitution to serve all students who walk through its doors.

Despite these differences, today's schools and many of today's firms face the same central problem: both must respond to a rapidly changing market and both must improve quality by developing and making use of the front-line workers. This common problem accounts for the emergence of common principles from the best schools and the best businesses.

In Chapters 4 through 7 we examine the first four principles, one at a time. Chapter 4 describes how T. A. Vasquez and the other parents at Zavala Elementary School worked with teachers to implement a more rigorous curriculum. But the parents could not support better education until they understood what the problem was.

Chapter 5 tells how Tony Barbosa, a student at Boston High School, found the right incentives as a participant in

Boston ProTech, a youth apprenticeship program. In many U.S. high schools, students have few incentives to take challenging courses. Boston ProTech and a modest number of other programs across the nation are working to provide strong incentives to students and to bridge the enormous gap between low-income inner-city schools and the big city white-collar employers.

Chapter 6 tells how fifth-grade teachers at Cabot Elementary School eventually got the training they needed to teach the physics of light through hands-on experiments. Chapter 7 describes how Vermont educators collaborated to devise new methods of assessing students' progress in acquiring communication and problem-solving skills.

All the stories recounted in these chapters demonstrate operation of the fifth principle: persevere and learn from mistakes. The stories show real people trying an idea, making mistakes, recovering, and ultimately finding better approaches. Chapter 8 discusses perseverance in greater detail and explains why the school reforms most advanced by politicians—more money, parental choice, charter schools, and national or statewide standards—are incomplete answers to the U.S. school problem. When they work, each of these reforms is a stimulus for change. None says anything about the form change should take. The stories in these chapters show that no change can raise student skills without doing the dirty work: the training of teachers, the organizing of parents, the restructuring of student incentives, the development of measures that will accurately chart progress.

The challenge of improving U.S. schools is difficult, but it can be met. As parental concern continues to grow, higher student skills will become an issue like smoking and diet and exercise: areas where great national changes are possible once people recognize the stakes and understand what to do. And like smoking and diet and exercise, parents who want better schools need not wait for some new state or national program. The process of teaching the New Basic Skills can occur—can only occur—on a school-by-school basis. Chapter 9 shows how committed people can begin this process.

A final point. In this book we argue that the most important problem U.S. schools face is preparing all children for tomorrow's jobs. As we make this argument, we recognize that some schools face the more immediate problem of establishing safety and order.

There is no simple pattern here. In the last 10 years, minority students have made significant gains in standardized test scores (Chapter 2). But for some children—minority and white—the trip from a poor neighborhood to the white-collar world remains an incredible journey. And in some schools, being able to go to the bathroom in safety is a precursor to interest in decimals and literature.

In the chapters that follow, we will show that progress is possible even in such schools when parents, students, and teachers know where they want to go and have the principles for getting there.

CHAPTER 2

SKILLS FOR A
MIDDLE-CLASS WAGE

W hat skills are needed today to get a good job?

In 1967, U.S. automakers built 29 million cars and trucks. Production work was physically hard but the pay was very good—over $32,000 per year in 1993 dollars. Hiring was fairly casual. Art Johnson, a human resource director at Ford Motor Company and an industry veteran, describes it as "the warm body process": "If we had a vacancy, we would look outside in the plant waiting room to see if there were any warm bodies standing there. If someone was there and they looked physically ok and they weren't an obvious alcoholic, they were hired."

By the mid-1980s, both the jobs and the employees were very different. General Motors, Ford, and Chrysler weren't hiring at all, and the new firms that were needed more than warm bodies.

HIRING AT DIAMOND-STAR MOTORS (DSM)

One of the new firms was Diamond-Star Motors, a joint venture of Mitsubishi of Japan (the diamond) and Chrysler

Motors (the star).[1] For Mitsubishi, the venture provided increased access to the U.S. market. For Chrysler, it was a way to learn the Japanese methods that were revolutionizing auto production. The new methods did not emphasize exotic robots; they emphasized new ways of using people. Frontline workers were no longer do-as-your-are-told warm bodies, but people with the skills and incentives to constantly improve their performance. The challenge was to select employees who could live up to this role.

The first DSM product was a two-seater sports coupe with three nameplates, the Plymouth Laser, the Mitsubishi Eclipse, and the Eagle Talon. The cars were built in a new plant located on farmland in Normal, Illinois. Management came from Mitsubishi and Chrysler, but the plant hired 2,900 new workers for two job titles: production associates, who did the bulk of assembly; and maintenance associates, who kept the plant's machinery and electronics in working order.

While DSM did not open as a unionized plant, it paid union wage rates, in 1987 about $27,000 per year, equivalent to about $33,000 in 1993 dollars, plus a strong benefits package. The salary was a little higher than what auto workers had made in 1967 (adjusted for inflation). By 1987, it was very good money for a man or woman who had not attended college. Eighty thousand people began the application process for DSM's 2,900 jobs, so DSM had a large pool from which to select the kind of workers it needed.

In conjunction with a New York–based personnel firm, DSM designed a list of skills that all DSM production and maintenance associates would need:

- The ability to read at a "high school level"
- The ability to do math at a "high school level"

- The ability to solve semistructured problems and to originate improvements (*Kaizen* in Japanese)
- The ability to work in teams
- Skills in oral communication
- Skills in inspection (the ability to detect errors)

The skills reflect the changing nature of production work. The warm bodies of 1967 were expected to perform a small number of routine operations—bolting a door to a frame—and nothing else. If an employee saw a better way of doing things, he kept his mouth shut. Improvements were management's job. If he saw a mistake or a problem, he would try to pass it on to the next work station. "Once you passed it on, it wasn't your problem anymore." As we will see later in this chapter, these routine jobs still exist, but they no longer pay a living wage.

In modern manufacturing, a production associate has a much wider scope of responsibility. He (or she) monitors the quality of the work passing through his area. When quality problems arise, he searches for solutions, often working with other associates. He is expected to offer frequent suggestions to improve performance.

This larger role means an employer must think carefully about who is hired. Diamond-Star's six skills represent an attempt to formalize this thinking. The last skill—inspection—is peculiar to production work. We will see that the first five skills are now demanded by high-wage firms throughout the economy.

To find people with these skills, Diamond-Star began its selection process with newspaper ads asking interested persons to contact the local office of the Illinois State Employment Service. There potential applicants were shown a 20-

minute video with scenes from a Mitsubishi automobile plant, describing what DSM would be like: the importance of being a team player, of working to solve problems, of offering suggestions to improve production, of putting the company's needs ahead of one's own in issues like accepting overtime. At several points the narrator asked potential job applicants to think hard about whether this was the type of job they wanted.

Most of the 80,000 applicants who showed up remained to fill out application forms containing questions about education and job history and then take the General Aptitude Test Battery (GATB). The GATB is a set of 12 standardized tests that takes about one hour to complete. It tests for nine different skills ranging from verbal and numerical aptitude to manual dexterity. DSM applicants received percentile scores describing their GATB performance relative to a national sample of workers of the same racial group and gender. If an applicant's scores exceeded preestablished cutoffs, which ranged between the fiftieth and seventieth percentiles on different aptitudes, the applicant moved on to a physical exam and drug testing.

Applicants who passed the physical exam and drug test were invited to DSM, where they took another standardized test, the Bennett Mechanical Comprehension Test, which assesses mechanical aptitude. The cutoff for this test—the fiftieth national percentile—eliminated 15 to 20 percent of the DSM applicants who took it.

Up to this point, DSM used pencil-and-paper multiple-choice tests, the scores on which are typically correlated with an IQ score. But "soft" skills like teamwork and the ability to communicate can't be measured by such tests. Now DSM turned to two expensive hands-on assessments.

In the first assessment each applicant was assigned to a small team composed of men and women with various ethnic backgrounds. After some icebreaking exercises, the team undertook a "board construction," in which it had to assemble circuit boards, wires, and modular components on a large frame according to a blueprint. The blueprint described the final product, but how the members of the team divided work and whether they helped each other out were left up to them. Trained assessors rated each person on oral communication, interpersonal skills, and problem-solving skills. When the board was built, the team held a *Kaizen* meeting to discuss how it might have done the job better. The team then assembled a second board. The whole exercise took 90 minutes.

The second assessment tested inspection skills. Individual applicants were brought into a room containing six different "nonsense models," each accompanied by a blueprint. Applicants were told that any of several things could be wrong with a model—the wrong-shaped head on a bolt, an incorrect number of washers, an incorrect part. An applicant had 105 seconds to study each model, identify any errors, and then move on to the next model. Applicants were rated in terms of the number of errors detected.

For applicants who obtained passing scores on the two assessments, the final step in the screening process was a half-hour interview with a panel of from three to 10 DSM production associates, supervisors, and general managers, who probed the "fit" between an applicant's skills and priorities and DSM's needs. Applicants' performance in this interview determined whether they were offered a job.

The people who designed DSM's selection procedure described it as a Cadillac operation (though Chrysler and

Mitsubishi might have used a different term). But other leading manufacturers, using less elaborate methods, look for
similar skills.

HIRING AT HONDA OF AMERICA MANUFACTURING (HAM)

Honda of America Manufacturing is headquartered in
Marysville, Ohio, where approximately 10,500 American
workers make Honda motorcycles and passengers cars.
Among the cars they make is the Accord, the largest-selling
car in America from 1989 through 1991. Unlike Diamond-
Star, Honda's compensation package includes a profit-shar-
ing component and a bonus for perfect attendance. But like
Diamond-Star, Honda's total compensation is well above the
$20,000 earned today by the average 30-year-old male high
school graduate, so Honda, too, can hire selectively from a
large number of applicants.

HAM's selection process differs from DSM's in details but
not in the end result. At the outset the employment department reviews a random selection of active applications, looking for warning signs like unanswered questions, the failure
to follow instructions, or an erratic work history. On the
basis of this review, between 10 and 25 percent of applicants
are invited to Marysville for testing and interviewing.

The day at Marysville includes a three-hour orientation
on the nature of work at Honda. As at DSM, applicants are
shown a video describing the firm's work environment,
which includes mandatory overtime work on some Satur-
days. Managers emphasize that new employees will work on
the evening shift for a long time, since most associates with
seniority prefer the day shift. During the orientation, appli-

cants are asked to think hard whether their skills and ambitions provide a good match with HAM's needs.

The day at Marysville continues with skill assessment, including a mathematics test, a reading test, and a safety inventory. The tests measure skills similar to those assessed by the General Aptitude Test Battery used by Diamond-Star. Honda's mathematics test measures skills taught no later than junior high school: the ability to convert fractions to percentages, the ability to interpret line graphs and bar graphs. Honda's reading test examines an applicant's ability to comprehend passages on topics like factory safety, teamwork, and quality and then to answer multiple-choice questions that require reading the passage closely but not interpreting it. The safety inventory is designed to evaluate the applicant's attitude toward safety. Most applicants who take the tests pass all three. Passing is all that counts: the margin by which someone passes is not considered. Diamond-Star treats GATB scores in the same way.

Applicants who pass the tests proceed to interviews that typically run 30 minutes each and are conducted by one person from HAM administration and one person from production. Interviewers look for an applicant's ability to communicate with others, for a sense of responsibility, for flexibility and a willingness to help others—for example, would an applicant be willing to temporarily drop his or her own work to help a co-worker who was having trouble? Many of the questions have no "right" answer. They are probes to assess how well an applicant would fit into the firm's work culture.

If the applicant is a recent high school graduate, the interviewers look for involvement in sports or student government or afterschool work—activities that HAM views as signs of motivation and initiative. Finally, HAM checks references from previous employers. The firm then makes employment offers to successful applicants, conditional upon a medical examination.

Both Diamond-Star and Honda are manufacturing firms. By the late 1980s, the search for skilled employees was equally advanced in service firms.

HIRING AT NORTHWESTERN MUTUAL LIFE (NML)

Northwestern Mutual Life Insurance Company is the seventh-largest life insurer in the nation. It specializes in life insurance, disability policies, and annuities. NML has operated in Milwaukee since 1857, where it now employs 3,000 people. Dubbed "The Quiet Company," NML has been financially conservative, keeping a low cost per policy and avoiding the real estate speculation of the 1980s. Like DSM and Honda, NML is viewed as one of the premiere employers in its area. It currently hires about 330 people per year from a pool of 7,000 applicants. DSM and Honda built themselves around new Japanese production processes. Northwestern Mutual Life *re*built itself around a new service production process—one that allowed one-stop shopping for consumers.

Until 1982 NML, like most of its competitors, organized work by function. An employee, for example, might be responsible for recording address changes for clients. Customers who requested other services were transferred to other employees. The narrowly defined jobs were the service-sector analog of bolting on car doors. The modest skills required for most jobs made NML a place where many enterprising high school graduates could find work. In 1980,

48 percent of the home office work force had no college education.

NML's work reorganization was driven by demographics. From the mid-1960s through the mid-1980s, the baby-boom cohorts were turning 21. From NML's perspective, these baby-boomers were large, automatic additions to the pool of life insurance customers. But after the mid-1980s the baby boom would be replaced by the baby bust, and companies like NML would have to work hard to maintain their customer base. Maintaining the customer base would require excellent customer service. But NML's work organization did not support excellent customer service because each employee could answer questions only in a narrow area, and customers calling in were often shunted from person to person or put on hold for extended periods.

Three decades ago, organization by function was the only way to get the work done. By the early 1980s, technological change, most notably the advent of more powerful computer hardware and software, made possible a new organization of work that provided clients with better service. With one of the best computer systems in the industry, NML was in a good position to take advantage of the new opportunities afforded by technological change.

In 1982 the firm reorganized, moving from a policy-based computer system to a client-based one. This change permitted every customer service representative to access on a computer screen information about all the policies held by an individual customer. The result was one-stop shopping: one telephone call got a representative who could answer almost any question on any of the customer's policies.

NML's reorganization to one-stop shopping has entailed both a major redesigning of jobs and major changes in the kinds of employee skills needed. Under the new system, a single customer service representative does a variety of tasks that previously had been carried out by several workers. Customer service representatives in the Policyowner Services Department had to become expert in the whole range of NML's policies, whereas before each had known about only one. The representatives had to know how to find answers to abstruse questions and how to deal with the concerns of sometimes irate clients. Under the previous form of organization, different NML employees had done each of these tasks—no one employee had to master them all.

NML responded to the increased need for skilled workers by hiring more college graduates. Over the decade from 1981 to 1991, the number of NML employees who had no formal education beyond high school remained stable at approximately 950. During the same period the number of employees with at least a four-year college degree doubled, from approximately 500 to more than 1,000.

The growing number of college graduates reflected two changes in NML's occupational structure. First was the increase in the number of employees in job categories that had traditionally required some college. Thus the number of underwriters, who usually have some college training, grew from 54 to 144 during the 1980s. Conversely, the number of typists and clerks, who usually have only high school diplomas, declined from 287 in 1981 to 152 in 1991. By itself the shift in NML's job structure was enough to shift the work force toward college graduates. But this shift was reinforced by a second change—the increasing tendency to hire persons with some college for jobs formerly held by high school graduates. Thus among customer service representatives the proportion who were four-year college graduates rose from 8 percent in 1981 to 20 percent in 1991. At first glance, these numbers suggest a surplus of college graduates pushing into "high school jobs." Later in the chapter we will see this is not the case. In both NML and national data, the skills required to do many "high school jobs" were rising and college graduates were being paid college-level wages to do them.

Clearly, reorganization resulted in more job opportunities for college-educated workers and fewer jobs paying middle-class wages for high school graduates. A review of their recruiting process explains why this happened.

NML's outside recruiting focuses on entry-level positions. More advanced positions are typically filled through internal promotion. Like Diamond-Star and Honda, NML expects most new employees to be with the firm for a long time. Consequently applicants are judged against two standards: the job for which they applied *and* the more advanced job they should be holding in two or three years.

In making these decisions, NML uses less formal procedures than Diamond-Star or Honda. Instead of administering cognitive tests to applicants, it relies on intensive interviewing, chiefly because communication skills are critical in most positions.

The process begins when an NML line manager receives authorization to add a new position. The manager then prepares a description of the job and the skills needed to perform it. If the position is to be filled from outside, the human resources office reviews existing applications. Candidates who appear to be good fits with the job description are asked to come for an interview. After screening by human resources personnel, applicants are interviewed by the line manager in the area with the job opening. It is this manager who makes the decision whether to hire the applicant.

Managers' interviews are conducted with established protocols that probe applicants' responses to open-ended questions, many of which deal with hypothetical work problems. The interviews also provide opportunities to assess foreign language skills, which NML officials feel will be increasingly important in the future. Here are some questions from the interviews for service correspondent:

> You've heard the expression "going the extra mile." Give me an example where you've done this in a work setting.
>
> If you could create a job tailored to you, what would that job entail?
>
> An agent calls and says that we took two monthly payments of $500 each from his client's checking account when we should have only drawn one. The agent is very upset and says that some of his client's checks are going to bounce because of the screwup. He demands to know who made the mistake. How would you respond?

Managers at NML offer various reasons for selecting college graduates instead of applicants with only a high school diploma. They say that college graduates tend to have better oral and written communication skills, and that they tend to learn about new products more quickly and have a broader view of the world. The managers emphasize that these are only tendencies, however; not all applicants with college degrees have these skills, nor do all applicants with only a high school education lack them. The personnel department tends to bypass applicants without college because today's high schools usually fail to teach these skills and the exceptions are hard to identify in interviews. When high school graduates are hired, they are usually individuals who had worked at NML while in high school as part of a cooperative education program, a program which provides supervisors a first-hand opportunity to observe a student at work.

What factors lead to an applicant's rejection? As at Diamond-Star and Honda, mastery of basic mathematics and literacy play some role in hiring. To explain why some applicants are rejected, NML managers offer summaries like "low grade-point average," "inadequate analytical or problem-solving skills," or "deficient in capacity to handle concepts." But here, as in the other two firms, interactive skills and attitudes toward work carry a lot of weight: rejected candidates have "poor communication skills," or were "not team players," "could not articulate clear goals," have "a questionable work ethic," or are "immature and/or lacking in self-confidence." And here, too, managers emphasize the importance of a work history giving evidence of reliability, stability, and relevant work experience.

THE NEW BASIC SKILLS

Hiring at Diamond-Star, Honda, and Northwestern Mutual is arduous, expensive, and highly selective. In most years no more than 10 percent of applicants are offered a job. But the most important feature of these hiring processes is that they are not unique. Over the last decade, more and more businesses have begun to look for a similar kind of worker. In addition to things that employers have always looked for— reliability, a positive attitude, and a willingness to work hard—these employers now look for hard and soft skills that applicants wouldn't have needed 20 years ago:

- The ability to read at the ninth-grade level or higher
- The ability to do math at the ninth-grade level or higher
- The ability to solve semistructured problems where hypotheses must be formed and tested
- The ability to work in groups with persons of various backgrounds
- The ability to communicate effectively, both orally and in writing
- The ability to use personal computers to carry out simple tasks like word processing

These are the New Basic Skills, the minimum skills people now need to get a middle-class job.

A surprise in the list of New Basic Skills is the importance of soft skills. The skills are called "soft" because they are not easily measured on standardized tests. In reality, there is nothing soft about them. Today more than ever, good firms expect employees to raise performance continually by learning from each other through written and oral communication and by group problem solving. For anyone who wants a job in a good firm, these soft skills are a necessity. Soft skills are not highly correlated with scores on pencil-and-paper IQ tests. If they were, firms would look for them by using multiple-choice tests rather than expensive hands-on simulations and interviews. In later chapters we show how some schools are learning how to teach these increasingly important soft skills.

A relatively new entry to the list of New Basic Skills is a rudimentary knowledge of computers. Diamond-Star and Honda do not require this knowledge of new workers, but NML requires word-processing skills for many entry-level jobs, and the demand for very basic computer skills is growing rapidly. In 1984, 26 percent of the work force used computers on the job. In 1993, the comparable figure was 48 percent.[2] Yet in 1992, more than half of U.S. high school seniors reported that they rarely or never used a personal computer, and only 25 percent reported using a personal computer at least once a week.[3] These figures suggest that a significant percentage of students leave high school without even elementary computer skills, and as a result are denied access to a growing number of jobs paying middle-class wages.

If the New Basic Skills appear surprisingly modest, recall that they are a floor. Many good jobs require greater skills, but very few require less. Doing math at a ninth-grade level means the ability to manipulate fractions and decimals and to interpret line graphs and bar graphs. It requires only a bare minimum of algebra. The fact that firms must test for this level of mathematical skill confirms the obvious: many recent high school graduates don't have it.

The same is true for other dimensions of the New Basic Skills. Solving a semistructured problem[4] requires formulating hypotheses and finding ways to test them. These are things that few schools teach. The same is true of working in teams and making effective oral presentations. But, as we demonstrate in later chapters, some schools do teach these skills, and all schools could.

HOW TODAY'S STUDENTS MEASURE UP

We know about students' math and reading skills because they are tested periodically by the National Assessment of Educational Progress (NAEP), a set of standardized tests administered roughly every four years to 31,000 nine-, 13-, and 17-year-olds drawn from a national sample of schools. On the basis of the passing scores on the written tests used by Diamond-Star and Honda (Northwestern Mutual did not use written tests), we can construct a rough equivalence between their basic requirements and NAEP scores: an applicant for a production associate's job would have to score roughly 300 points or higher on both the math and reading tests to meet either company's cutoffs (Table 2.1).

How many 17-year-olds meet this standard? A score of 300 is close to the national average in both reading and math. On the 1992 NAEP math test, three out of five 17-year-olds scored 300 or more. On the NAEP reading test, only two out of five scored 300 or more.[5] This is a sobering

Table 2.1
Interpreting the NAEP Scores

Math score range = 0–500

200 = Can add and subtract two-digit numbers and recognize relationships among coins

250 = Can add, subtract, multiply, and divide using whole numbers and solve one-step problems

300 = Can compute with decimals, fractions, and percentages; recognize geometric figures; solve simple equations; and use moderately complex reasoning

350 = Can solve multistep problems and use beginning algebra

Reading score range = 0–500

200 = Can comprehend specific or sequentially related information

250 = Can search for specific information, interrelate ideas, and make generalizations

300 = Can find, understand, summarize, and explain relatively complicated information

350 = Can synthesize and learn from specialized reading materials

---

picture: close to half of all 17-year-olds cannot read or do math at the level needed to get a job in a modern automobile plant. Barring some other special knowledge or talent that would allow them to earn a living as, say, a plumber or an artist, they lack the skills to earn a middle-class paycheck in today's economy.

If today's low NAEP scores showed a fast-rising trend, the problem would be less serious. But that is not the case. Over the last 10 years, NAEP math scores have risen moderately, but reading scores have not. For the last 20 years, the picture is slightly brighter, with moderate increases in both reading and math. The gains have been concentrated among minority students (Table 2.2). But despite the moderate closing of the test score gap between minority students and white students, black and Hispanic students are still much

Table 2.2

Average NAEP Reading and Math Scores, 1982 and 1992

	Age 9		Age 17	
	1982	1992	1982	1992
Mathematics				
All	219	230	289	307
White	224	235	304	312
Black	195	208	272	286
Hispanic	204	212	277	292
Reading				
All	211	210	289	290
White	218	218	295	297
Black	186	184	264	261
Hispanic	187	192	258	271

Source: Ina V. S. Mullis et al., *Report in Brief: NAEP 1992 Trends in Academic Progress* (Washington, D.C.: National Center for Education Statistics), 1994, table 6, p. 17.

more likely than white students to enter the labor force without mastery of the New Basic Skills.

VALIDATING THE SKILLS

Diamond-Star, Honda, Northwestern Mutual, and a growing number of other firms know what they want. But do they know what they are doing? Evidence that they do comes from a validity study of DSM's recruiting methods conducted by the New York–based personnel firm that established DSM's selection process. The study examined the correlation between an employee's on-the-job performance, as rated by supervisors, and the employee's performance on each aspect of the selection process—the GATB tests, the mechanical aptitude test, the assessment simulations, and the interviews. The findings illustrate the importance of soft skills in today's economy.

The study's most striking findings involved employee scores on the GATB, the multiple-choice test of nine skills ranging from verbal and numerical aptitude to manual dexterity. Applicants had to have GATB scores above a fixed threshold to move to the next stage in the selection process. But the margin by which scores were above the threshold had almost no relationship to job performance. By contrast, applicants' scores both on assessment exercises and in interviews were better predictors of on-the-job performance. Neither the assessment scores nor the interview scores were highly correlated with scores on the GATB.

These patterns suggest that DSM and similar firms are selecting applicants in roughly the right way, while avoiding two mistakes. One mistake would be to set much higher cognitive thresholds—to require, for example, that applicants be able to work trigonometry problems. Such skills might result in modestly higher performance but they would encounter diminishing returns in the form of a smaller and higher-priced applicant pool.[6]

The other mistake would be to assume that all important skills can be measured with paper-and-pencil tests. The Diamond-Star validity study suggests just the opposite: once reading and math scores on paper-and-pencil tests are above a certain threshold, the soft skills—teamwork and communication skills—are the best predictors of performance, and these cannot be detected on multiple-choice tests.

The DSM validation sheds light on the recently resurgent controversy of whether IQ is all that matters in the labor market. If IQ were the dominant factor determining on-the-job performance, we would expect that scores on the IQ-like GATB test would be highly correlated with supervisor ratings. The actual pattern at DSM was quite different: once applicants scored above a threshold, supervisor ratings were best predicted by scores on soft-skill assessments, scores that were quite *un*correlated with the GATB scores. This pattern suggests that employee performance and wages depend on several factors, only some of which are closely linked to IQ.

NATIONWIDE TRENDS

The examples of Northwestern Mutual Life, Diamond-Star, and Honda of America illustrate dimensions of a two-pronged increase in the demand for skills. One, evident at NML though not at the automotive manufacturers, is a shift in demand toward college graduates and away from high school graduates. The other, discussed shortly, is a greater demand for cognitive and interactive skills *among* workers with the same level of formal education. If these trends were confined to a few best-practice firms, they would offer little guidance to schools. But, in fact, both trends can be seen in national data sets.

Figure 2.1 shows the trend in earnings for college and high school graduates over the last 15 years—men and women in their late twenties and early thirties. The picture is clear: among women, the earnings of college graduates rose sharply while those of high school graduates declined slightly. Among men, the earnings of college graduates declined slightly while those of high school graduates declined sharply. Among both women and men, the earnings gap between college and high school graduates increased to levels not seen since the late 1930s.[7] As we show below, a part of this shift reflects employer demand for what is learned in college. But a greater part reflects employer demand for the basic skills of those who go to college, skills these students mastered before they set foot on campus and skills that could be taught to most students.

Some observers have advanced a different view—that the country suffers from a surplus of well-educated workers and that college graduates are increasingly forced to take "high school jobs"—not upgraded high school jobs like a Northwestern Mutual Life customer service representative, but true high school jobs in which college graduates are overqualified and underpaid.[8] The data in Figure 2.1 rule out this notion. If large numbers of college graduates were in true high school jobs, they would have been earning high school wages, and the college-high school earnings gap

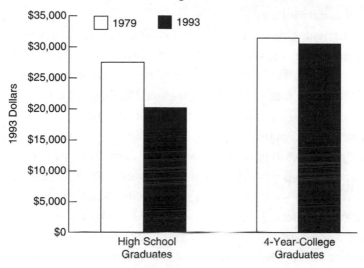

Median Earnings of 25- to 34-Year-Old Men

☐ 1979　■ 1993

1993 Dollars

High School Graduates　4-Year-College Graduates

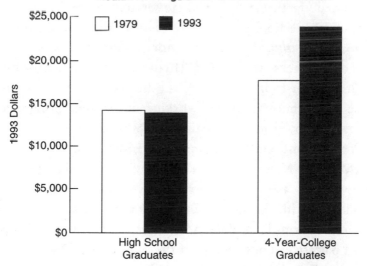

Median Earnings of 25- to 34-Year-Old Women

☐ 1979　■ 1993

1993 Dollars

High School Graduates　4-Year-College Graduates

Figure 2.1

would have grown smaller over the 1980s instead of widening dramatically.

The widening college–high school earnings gap shows that statements about skill upgrading by firms like NML are not just rhetoric. By shifting employment to college graduates, NML had to hire relatively high-priced college graduates even as high school graduates were available for less and less money. NML managers justified the shift by arguing that college graduates tended to have better command of the New Basic Skills—particularly stronger communication skills and writing skills—and they had an easier time learning the details of new products. These tendencies were strong enough to produce a substantial shift in the firm's labor force.

What was true for NML in this regard was true for the country as a whole. The weak earnings of high school graduates were not just the result of a shift of jobs from high-wage manufacturing to low-wage services. Rather, the earnings of high school graduates fell *within* the manufacturing sector and *within* the service sector as demand for less-educated workers weakened throughout the economy. Expressed in today's dollars, the hourly wages of young male high school graduates working in manufacturing were 14 percent lower in 1993 than in 1979.[9]

The second shift in demand is illustrated by DSM's, HAM's, and NML's use of tests, hands-on simulations, and interviews to assess mastery of the New Basic Skills among applicants with the same number of years of schooling. In economic terms, this demand translates into a straightforward pattern: among people of the same age and education, those with the higher cognitive and interactive skills get the higher wages.

A recent set of interviews with 56 firms located in the

Los Angeles and Detroit metropolitan areas supports the evidence from Honda, Diamond-Star, and NML. More than 60 percent of the managers reported that skill requirements in their organizations are increasing for entry-level jobs; more than 80 percent report that the jobs require basic literacy or math, and that soft skills are among the most important hiring criteria.[10]

Further confirmation comes from analyses of national data sets. There are no national data sets with quantitative measures of soft skills—interactive skills cannot be assessed by paper-and-pencil tests. But such tests can assess cognitive skills like basic math knowledge, and national data sets that measure these skills reenforce the picture: mastery of basic cognitive skills is associated with higher wages, and this association has grown stronger over time.

Evidence comes from two nationwide longitudinal surveys sponsored by the U.S. Department of Education. In the first, begun in 1972, more than 20,000 high school seniors completed a battery of tests assessing reading and mathematical skills. The math test focused on students' ability to read well enough to follow directions, manipulate and use fractions and decimals, and interpret graphs; it did not assess mastery of more advanced mathematics, such as algebraic problem solving or probability theory. In terms of difficulty, the questions were similar to those in the GATB test battery, used by Diamond-Star, and in Honda's own math screening test. Table 2.3 provides examples of test questions. In 1978, the Department of Education interviewed those who had taken the tests, recording any subsequent college education and their experiences in the labor market. In 1980 another nationwide sample of high seniors took essentially the same tests, with follow-interviews occurring in 1986.[11]

Table 2.3

A Sample of Test Items from the U.S. Department of Education

Mathematics Examination Administered to Samples

of High School Seniors in 1972 and 1980

Directions: Each problem consists of two quantities, one placed in Column A and one in Column B. You are to compare the two quantities and circle the letter

    A if the quantity in Column A is greater;
    B if the quantity in Column B is greater;
    C if the two quantities are equal;
    D if the size relationship cannot be determined from the information given.

	Column A	*Column B*	
1.	Length represented by 3 inches on a scale of 4 feet to an inch	A length of 12 feet	A B C D
2.	$\frac{1}{Q} = \frac{3}{4}$	$\frac{1}{P} = \frac{4}{3}$	
	Q	P	A B C D
3.	Cost per apple at a rate of $2.00 per dozen apples	Cost per apple at a rate of 3 apples for $0.50	A B C D
4.	245	$2(10)^3 + 4(10)^2 + 5(10)$	A B C D

Using these two longitudinal surveys, we can test the proposition that a young person's mastery of basic skills was a more important determinant of subsequent wages in the mid-1980s than in the late-1970s.[12] To do this, we first examined the importance of high school seniors' math scores in predicting hourly wages six years after high school graduation (when the graduates were 24), focusing on high school

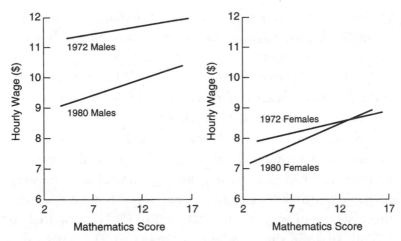

Figure 2.2 Fitted Relationship Between Hourly Wage (in 1993 $) at Age 24 and Mathematics Score at Age 17, by Year of High-School Graduation

graduates who did not go to college. Figure 2.2 shows the results, expressed in 1993 dollars.

Two of the patterns shown in Figure 2.2 confirm those in Figure 2.1: hourly wages for 24-year-old male high school graduates were lower in 1986 than in 1978, and in each year females earned less than males. The upward slope of all the lines illustrates that graduates with mastery of basic mathematics earned higher wages at age 24 than did graduates with weaker math skills. The steeper slopes of the lines for the 1980 graduates also show that these skills were stronger determinants of wages for the later group. Specifically, 24-year-old males in 1978 who had not gone to college but had a strong grasp of basic mathematical skills earned an average of $11.88 per hour (all wages in 1993 dollars). Their peers who had graduated from high school with weak math skills—unable to use fractions and decimals in simple problem solving—earned $11.30 per hour. Thus, in 1978 the ability to follow directions and to manipulate fractions and decimals affected wages six years after graduation only modestly—about 60 cents per hour, or $1,200 per year. In 1986, the difference between strong and weak basic math skills translated into a wage difference of $1.33 per hour, or about $2,700 per year for male high school graduates.

For females, basic mathematical skills were even more important determinants of wages. In 1978, 24-year-old women who had graduated from high school with mastery of basic math skills earned 93 cents per hour more than those who had very weak math skills ($8.81 compared to $7.88). In 1986 this gap had expanded to $1.71 per hour ($8.90 compared to $7.19), or about $3,400 per year.[13]

The relationships shown in Figure 2.2 are drawn from nationally representative samples of young workers. The patterns are very similar when students' scores on a test of reading comprehension replace the math scores in the analysis. These results demonstrate that in the economy as a whole, mastery of basic cognitive skills plays a larger role than it did 20 years ago in determining which high school graduates are able to find jobs by their midtwenties that pay middle-class wages.

The same two national data sets allow us to answer the question raised earlier in this chapter: How much of the growth in the college–high school wage gap reflects differences at high school graduation between the skills of people who enter college and those who don't? (The alternative hypothesis is that growth in the wage differential reflects the growing value of skills learned in college.) Between 1978 and 1986 the differential between the wages of 24-year-old women with a four-year B.A and those with only a high school diploma increased by 20 percent.[14] But as we have seen, some fraction of this premium reflects employer demand for young people with strong basic skills—skills they had before they entered college. We can capture this fraction by statistically controlling for each woman's score on the mathematics test taken as a high school senior. When this adjustment is made, there is *no growth* between 1978 and 1986 in the college wage premium for women.

The pattern for males, while less dramatic, is still quite strong. Between 1978 and 1986, the college–high school wage premium for 24-year-old men doubled. When the high school math score is controlled, the growth is cut by more than one-third.

These statistical results complement the stories of Diamond-Star, Honda, and NML. Between 1978 and 1986 (and continuing through today) it became more important to high-wage employers that workers possess mastery of a set of basic skills. A firm could screen for these skills by using extensive tests and assessments. This is what Diamond-Star and Honda did. The more common way to screen was to hire college graduates since high school students who finished college tended to be those with strong basic skills. This is what NML did. To be sure, people learn things in college that employers value. This explains why a 24-year-old college graduate earns more than a 24-year-old high school graduate when both had the same math score as high school seniors. But the *growth* in the college wage premium between 1978 and 1986 reflects, in large part, the growing importance of basic cognitive skills taught in high school.

Is college a necessary ticket to today's middle class? All of these results suggest the answer is no. A more effective solution to the demand for skilled labor involves improving elementary and high school education so that all students master the New Basic Skills and can demonstrate this mastery to employers. College will continue to be a good investment for a great many Americans in the years ahead. But with improvements in K–12 education, an expensive college education need not be the only way to obtain a middle-class job.

PROSPECTS FOR UNSKILLED WORKERS

Where did the changes of the 1980s leave us? During that decade, as high school graduates' earnings fell, it became fashionable to argue that the country faced a skills shortage that was limiting national economic growth and competitiveness. By the mid-1990s it was clear that this prophecy was off the mark. Beginning in 1992, economic growth was brisk and labor productivity began to grow strongly after a 20-year hiatus. In both 1994 and 1995, the World Economic Forum ranked the United States as the world's most competitive economy.[15] But as Figure 2.1 makes clear, the new competitiveness did not benefit everyone. This is the real danger of low worker skills: that economic growth can proceed while leaving large numbers of workers behind. To understand today's market for unskilled workers, consider the hiring process at Sports Plus.

Sports Plus is a family-owned sporting goods wholesaler that has been in business for 30 years. It is located in a city that has traditionally been the first home for waves of new immigrants. Many of the city's firms, including Sports Plus, utilize immigrant labor.

Sports Plus is a wholesaler, not a producer. Virtually all its goods are now produced in southeast Asia by low-wage subcontractors. The firm's central goal is to keep costs low.

As one manager said, "We don't produce anything that people really need. Most purchases are impulse buying. Price matters." Sports Plus employs 160 people belonging to three categories: office staff and administration (60), assemblers (70), and pickers (30). Of these workers, the assemblers are the least skilled.

Assemblers put together the parts of items like badminton sets. The work is very unskilled—training requires about 15 minutes—and many of the jobs are filled by day laborers—primarily Vietnamese workers brought to the firm by van from a nearby urban center. The independent labor contractor who hires the day laborers is a Vietnamese man who worked in the plant as a day laborer several years ago. He now comes in his Mercedes to pick up his check. The personnel director at Sports Plus once asked him how he manages always to find the number of workers that the plant has requested. He said that in fact he has several thousand people who want to work and who are available on call.

Sports Plus assembly workers begin at $5.50 per hour. Their wages can rise to a maximum of $7.00 per hour, a rate reserved for a few people who have been with the firm for many years. Although turnover is very high, some assembly workers have been with the firm for several years. Most of these employees are women for whom the firm arranges flexible hours. When longtime workers ask why they are not paid more, the company responds by pointing to the unskilled nature of the work: a longtime worker can be immediately replaced by someone who would start at $5.50 and within half a day could do the work equally well.

The company's 30 "picker" jobs require somewhat higher skills. A picker packages customer orders. If K mart

wants 90 balls, and balls are packed six to each master carton, the picker must be able to figure out that 15 master cartons are needed to fill the order. Pickers must know how to
read and to do elementary arithmetic. Pickers' wages start at
$6.35 per hour and extend to $7.35.

When Sports Plus hires an assembler, it uses the equiva-
lent of the warm-body process. The personnel director con-
ducts a short interview to assess whether the applicant can
get along with other workers. Punctuality, regular attendance, and the ability to get along are all that are required.
In fact, punctuality is so important that the firm gives two
movie tickets to every hourly employee who is not tardy or
absent for a month, five tickets after three months, and $100
for perfect attendance with no tardiness for a year. A worker
who is absent four times without a medical certificate and
proper notification is fired.

Because pickers need some mathematics skills, their hiring process is more formal. First, they must complete an
employment application form that asks for name, address,
phone number, and information about their last three jobs
and any military service. Many of the immigrants cannot fill
out the application form and are thereby immediately
screened out. Because the job requires lifting order cartons,
applicants are next asked to pick up a 100-pound box.
Finally, applicants are given a 20-item test of arithmetic
skills, involving addition, subtraction, multiplication, and
division of whole numbers. Eight of the problems are word
problems, the remaining 12 are simple computations. None
involves fractions or decimals. The problems in Table 2.4 are
taken from the Sports Plus math test for pickers.

Among applicants who speak English, 75 percent get 18

Table 2.4

Questions from the Sports Plus Test for Applicants for the Picker Job

Circle the correct answer to each question:

1. A customer has ordered 48 soccer balls, Item #18784. Item #18784 is packed 6 balls to each carton. How many cartons will you have to pick to fill the customer's order?

    A. 8   B. 6   C. 7   D. 10

2. If there are 2,119 items in a carton and you subtracted 143 items from the carton, how many would be left?

    A. 2,000   B. 1,971   C. 1,976   D. 1,791

---

out of 24 items right, and 10 percent get them all right. Most non-English-speakers do not try the test. Those who do tend to get the computation items correct but not the word problems, a score that still may qualify them for a job.

Both assemblers and pickers face the same prospects: little room for higher wages and no job ladders to climb. The result is very high turnover, even among pickers. Sports Plus's personnel director estimates that only half the pickers he hires stay for more than two weeks.

Some observers argue that in today's economy, people without skills won't have jobs. This is certainly true in some locations, especially inner-city neighborhoods.[16] But the general proposition is incorrect. The jobs will usually be there, but at very low wages. As the excess supply of unskilled workers has grown, their wages have continued to decline. In 1993 dollars, the hourly starting wage for assembly workers at Sports Plus was $6.52 in 1972, $6.12 in 1982, and $5.50 in 1993. The ability to do very basic math, a skill not all workers have, provides a small increase in wage, with pickers earning 90 cents per hour more than assemblers. But even someone with these elementary skills is not earning anything like what it takes to support a family. Pickers who work year-round full-time (fifty 40-hour weeks) earn $13,300, an income below the poverty line for a family of four.

The fact that Sports Plus hires immigrants is not unusual: immigrants now account for about one-fifth of all workers in the United States who are high school dropouts.[17] By contributing to the supply of unskilled workers to firms like Sports Plus, the immigration of workers with little schooling has contributed modestly to a decline in the earnings of high school dropouts and graduates. But the bulk of that decline stems from long-term economic changes coming from technology and trade—changes that will continue into the foreseeable future.

THE MISSION FOR SCHOOLS

From Diamond-Star to Sports Plus to national data sets, the evidence in this chapter has told a single story: The U.S. economy is changing rapidly in ways that have disastrous consequences for workers who lack the New Basic Skills— skills that were unnecessary for many good jobs even 15 years ago. There are the "hard" skills, including the ability to do basic mathematics and to understand written instructions. There are the "soft" skills, including the ability to communicate clearly and to work productively in groups to solve problems. And there are elementary computer skills.

Here is the dilemma. While the New Basic Skills are increasingly necessary for economic success, almost half the nation's 17-year-olds leave high school without them. In the next chapter we show how principles discovered by best-practice firms in their efforts to effectively manage skilled labor offer a framework for helping schools to accomplish their most central mission—providing all students with the New Basic Skills.

CHAPTER 3

FIVE PRINCIPLES FOR MANAGING FRONTLINE WORKERS

MANAGING ALBERT EINSTEIN

How do you manage people with the New Basic Skills? The question is important. Suppose that Albert Einstein had been hired as an assembler at Sports Plus, the sporting-goods wholesaler described in Chapter 2. What would he have earned? Einstein personified brilliance, but there is no evidence that he could assemble badminton sets faster than the average assembler. Since the assembler's job offers no scope for brilliance, Einstein would have earned the same $5.50 to $7.00 per hour earned by his co-workers.

Managers in best-practice firms stay up late wrestling with the Einstein Problem. Their firms use expensive recruiting procedures to hire workers with the New Basic Skills, and the firms pay high wages. But all this money is wasted unless managers design jobs that give workers the opportunities and incentives to put their skills to use.

In this chapter we return to Honda of America and Northwestern Mutual Life to see how skilled workers are managed. Although the details differ, these firms design their jobs using five broad principles meant to foster the performance of frontline workers. We show these principles in action and illustrate how they enable workers with the New Basic Skills to improve the performance of their organizations.

We also show why there is a compelling case for using these Five Principles in improving schools. In management terms, fostering the motivation and development of frontline workers in businesses is similar to fostering the motivation and development of teachers and students and parents in schools. Thus, the Five Principles provide an action plan for schools as they reorganize to teach the New Basic Skills.

THE STOPPED BLOWER NUT

When Honda hired Bill Bourbeau, he had the New Basic Skills: solid literacy, command of basic mathematics, the ability to communicate and work with a variety of people, an interest in solving problems. After graduating from high school in Virginia in 1965, he spent four years in the Air Force, followed by 17 years working in manufacturing firms. Laid off from Martin Marietta, Bourbeau came to Ohio to look for work. On the advice of friends, he applied for a job at Honda and in September 1988 began work on the second shift, installing heaters on Accords.

Diann Buckner graduated from high school in Ohio in 1982 and went to work at Wendy's, where she rose to become a store manager. In the spring of 1986 Buckner applied for work at Honda, largely because of Honda's higher pay. In November 1986 she began work on the second shift, installing heater controls, air vents, and radios on the instrument panels of Accords.

By 1990 both Bourbeau and Buckner had moved to the first shift, installing heaters and blowers in four-door Accords. They attached these parts by screwing six-millimeter nuts onto studs protruding from the frame. In talking with co-workers on their team, they realized that they all were experiencing difficulties attaching the nuts securely to the upper-dash studs. In August 1990 Bourbeau, Buckner, and two co-workers, Rick Russell and Pat Burns, decided to form a New Honda (NH) Circle, a "quality circle" in management language, to diagnose and solve the problem. Management supported their proposal, and the group, which named itself the Sharpshooters, started to meet for one hour each week on company time. After drawing up an activity plan with a schedule, they got down to work.

The Sharpshooters first identified the different upper-dash stud problems they were encountering and used checksheets to record the frequency with which each problem appeared over a five-day period. Using the checksheets, they constructed a Pareto diagram (Figure 3.1), a quality-control bar graph used to prioritize problems. The data showed that the most prevalent upper-stud problem was a stopped blower nut, a nut that couldn't be screwed completely onto the blower stud. When the nuts couldn't be fastened securely, the blowers couldn't be tightly fitted to the chassis of the Accord. To deal with a stopped blower nut, an associate removed it and tried to screw it on again. If several attempts failed to secure a tight fit, the associate used a die to rethread the stud. All of these remedies slowed production, and the rush to catch up jeopardized quality.

The Sharpshooters' goal was to eliminate stopped blower nuts. Meeting once a week from 3:00 to 4:00 P.M., a paid overtime hour, the group created cause-and-effect diagrams

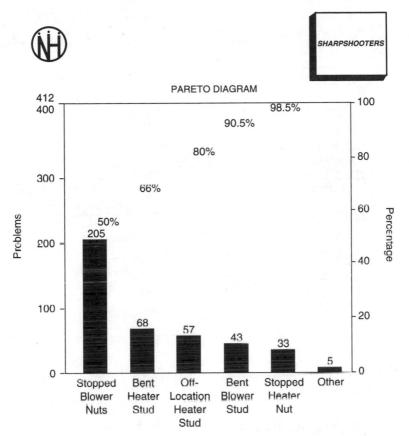

Figure 3.1 Honda Sharpshooters' Pareto Diagram

(Figure 3.2) to organize possible causes, then collected data to test the various possible explanations. Using Pareto charts and histograms, they concluded that the problem stemmed from an excess accumulation of paint on the studs when the chassis passed through the paint shop.

Step by step, the Sharpshooters pursued the source of the problem. Why had the excess paint appeared only in recent months? Again they listed potential explanations including

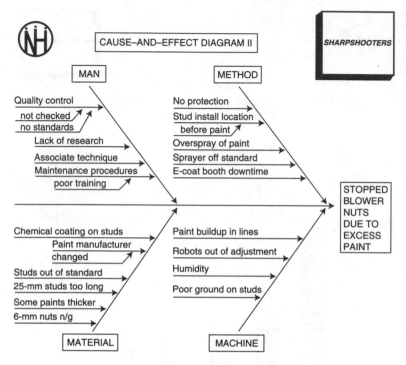

Figure 3.2   Honda Sharpshooters' Cause-and-Effect Diagram

changes in paint composition and in the programming of the painting robots. Pursuing each alternative, they discovered that the problem stemmed from an engineering change made several months earlier in order to attach the heater more securely to the Honda chassis. A 20-millimeter stud had been replaced by a 25-millimeter one, and paint was collecting on the additional threads of the longer stud.

Having identified the problem, the Sharpshooters turned to solutions. They brainstormed for alternative strategies using cause-and-effect diagrams to organize ideas. One possibility, they thought, was to have production associates in the paint department wipe off the excess paint on the stud before the body paint was baked dry. The group devised a plan to test the solution and then presented both the problem and the solution to the paint department coordinator. The coordinator agreed to the test, and paint department production associates tried the solution for four hours. The solution didn't work: it was hard to reach and wipe the studs without touching other freshly painted areas.

The Sharpshooters devised and tested five more solutions before they found one that worked: covering the studs with masking tape before the body was painted, and removing the tape just before the body entered the assembly department. On March 21, 1991, eight months after the Sharpshooters began their work, management added the masking-tape step to the procedure used to paint all Accords at Honda of America.

The stopped blower nut is a story about Honda's management of skilled workers to pursue the firm's goals of higher quality and lower cost. An inexpensive stud whose threads were clogged with paint was causing an expensive problem. Ignore the nut and the heater blower would rattle, undermining Honda's reputation for quality and, ultimately, Honda's sales. Rework each stud by hand and the production line would slow, raising production costs. The best solution was to fix manufacturing procedures so that stopped nuts did not occur. But who could design the fix?

Honda's production associates were the obvious candidates—they were, after all, closest to the problem—but giving them the job required satisfying a number of conditions. Production associates had to have an interest in solving the problem. They had to have the skills to define the problem precisely and to test alternative explanations. They needed the time and authority to test solutions that would involve workers in other parts of the production process. They had to be able to measure the progress they were making. They had to present their work convincingly to others.

Not all jobs have these conditions. The Sports Plus assembler's job has none of them. Sports Plus makes money by assembling simple, standardized products in routine ways and selling them at low prices. In their case, raising wages to attract workers with the New Basic Skills makes no economic sense.

In contrast, Honda management created the conditions that encouraged and supported the work of the Sharpshooters because they promote Honda's business strategy, which might be summarized in the following way:

Competitive advantage comes from continuous improvement in quality and cost. The frontline workers in the assembly, welding, painting, and stamping departments see things every day that affect quality and cost. Enlisting these men and women in identifying and solving problems is the key to continuous improvement.

In 1991, the Sharpshooters were one of 200 quality circles formed to solve specific problems. And the logic of their approach applies as much to services as it does to manufacturing.

THE UNDERWRITER'S WORKBENCH

Karen Pawlak went to work at the central office of Northwestern Mutual Life in downtown Milwaukee right after graduating from high school in 1973. In 1972, NML looked for new graduates who seem to be reliable and willing to work hard and to learn. The firm put them into simple jobs and watched for potential. Karen Pawlak's first job at NML was delivering messages and documents in the actuarial department. She then moved to a position coding changes in customers' policies. Pawlak had the skills to advance, and today, 23 years after starting work at NML, she is a senior disabilities underwriter.

Underwriting is the core of NML's work. Each year, 300,000 applications for life and disability insurance come to NML's home office from independent insurance agents. At any time, Karen is reviewing 120 of these applications for disability insurance. She must gather and evaluate evidence from medical records, physicians' statements, lab studies, and tax returns. She communicates on specific cases with physicians and finance experts. She must collect and integrate medical and financial information to determine an applicant's risk of disability: whether NML should write a policy and, if so, what the premium should be. If she is too liberal, claims will exceed premiums and profits will decline. If she is too cautious, she will drive profitable business to competitors and infuriate the independent agents on whom NML depends for business.[1]

Unlike many jobs, that of underwriter has always required extensive skills and initiative. But in recent years, the processes involved in Karen Pawlak's job have changed significantly as a result of computerization. Computerization required that Pawlak learn new skills. It also required that NML management learn to work with underwriters to make a new system useful.

Until the late 1980s, NML underwriters worked with paper files, each containing an application and its supporting material. When an underwriter approved an application and determined the premium, the file work was passed to lower-level employees who sent the approval letters to the agent and the applicant. Since all material was in paper files, information was sometimes hard to locate, and responses to inquiries from agents were sometimes delayed.

In the late 1980s, NML began to develop and implement the Underwriters' Workbench, a computerized support system that would put an application and supporting material on-line. Using Workbench underwriters would also generate the letters to applicants and agents that had previously been produced by other NML employees. Karen and the other men and women in her unit would move from underwriters per se to case managers. Like other job changes within NML, it was a move toward one-stop shopping to provide both agents and individual customers with better service.

In theory Workbench had obvious advantages: an underwriter sitting at a networked personal computer could quickly access an application to answer an agent's inquiry; lab results needed to evaluate an application could be sent electronically from the NML lab to the underwriter's PC; errors would be reduced because instead of passing among several employees, an application would be handled by a single underwriter all the way through policy issuance. The plan was to have four underwriters begin piloting the system in August 1988 and to have all underwriters on the system by 1991.

No one thought that implementing Workbench would be easy. Workbench would be the first NML system based on networked personal computers. It had to win the confidence of the underwriters, highly skilled workers who were used to dealing with large paper files, but were not used to communicating with anxious agents. It would change the job

descriptions of the lower-level workers who had been handling the communication. And all these changes could not be
allowed to seriously disrupt NML's basic work.

Workbench proved even harder to implement than
expected. The first software did not provide rapid responses
to underwriters' queries and so left them frustrated. Some
underwriters balked at now having to handle communications and letter writing. By 1990 even the pilot program was
still not complete and Workbench was probably lowering
the productivity of those who were using it.

But the people at NML understood that few changes—
including changes for the better—work the first time. Managers began to work more closely with Karen Pawlak and
the other underwriters to redesign processes. New, more
rapid software was purchased. The implementation schedule
was expanded to provide more time for underwriter training
and for software fine-tuning.

By the summer of 1995, NML was close to its goals. All
underwriters were using Workbench, although some were
still receiving training. Computer systems specialists continued to work with underwriters to remove remaining bugs.
Although implementation was not complete, Workbench
had become a way of life at NML, and the benefits of cost
reduction and speedier policy issuance were finally visible.

The Underwriters' Workbench, like the stopped blower
nut, is a story about managing skilled workers to pursue
organizational goals—in NML's case, improving customer
service. One major ingredient in the effort's success has been
organizational perseverence. Workbench will ultimately pay
big dividends, but those dividends were far from evident in
the first two years. Had NML managers been looking for a
quick fix, they would have simply scrapped the project.

Another major ingredient was the ability of NML managers to change their management style. Initially, managers viewed Workbench implementation as a top-down process. They saw underwriters as skilled workers but not as software experts. In management's view, most communication would run in one direction, from the software people and trainers to the underwriters. That process led to gridlock. Only after managers began to actively solicit the underwriters' ideas and participation did the implementation really start to move.

FIVE PRINCIPLES FOR MANAGING SKILLED WORKERS

Honda of America and Northwestern Mutual Life differ in many respects. One manufactures; the other provides financial services. NML has an employees' union, Honda does not. All Honda workers, from the president to the newest associate, wear the same white uniforms with first names embroidered above the right pocket; they eat in the same cafeterias and park in the same lots. NML has more organizational levels and a wood-paneled dining room for entertaining guests.

Yet the two firms are similar in their approach to the market. Both see continually improving the quality of their products and controlling costs as keys to their long-term success. Both recognize that technological changes, especially the advent of computers, create new possibilities for organizing production. Both have committed themselves to providing the training needed to make the new jobs "doable." Finally, both firms recognize that the employees who do the work see things every day that affect quality and cost, and that a powerful strategy for improving quality and controlling cost is to design the organization so as to encourage workers to detect problems, point them out, and play a key role in their solution.

The common core of the Honda and NML management style is summarized in Five Principles:

1. Ensure that all frontline workers understand the problem.
2. Design jobs so that all frontline workers have both incentives and opportunities to contribute to solutions.
3. Provide all frontline workers with the training needed to pursue solutions effectively.
4. Measure progress on a regular basis.
5. Persevere and learn from mistakes; there are no magic bullets.

The Five Principles are interdependent. Training makes no sense if workers have no opportunity to use newly acquired skills. An organization cannot design good incentives if its goals are unclear. Effective problem solving takes time and requires persistence in the face of initial setbacks.

At first glance, the Five Principles seem to be common sense. But they are a radical departure from Frederick W. Taylor's principles of scientific management, the dominant U.S. management philosophy for most of this century. Taylor's philosophy was top-down. He believed that scientific study by management experts—time-and-motion studies—would uncover the one best way to do any job. The workers' responsibility was to adopt the expert's solution. Taylor's instructions to a pig-iron carrier named Schmidt vividly convey his approach:

Well, if you are a high-priced man, you will do exactly as this man tells you to-morrow, from morning till night. When he tells you to pick up a pig and walk, you pick it up and you walk, and when he tells you to sit down and rest, you sit down. You do that right straight through the day. And what's more, no back talk. Now a high-priced man does just what he's told to do, and no back talk. Do you understand that? When this man tells you to walk, you walk; when he tells you to sit down, you sit down, and you don't talk back to him. Now you come on to work to-morrow morning and I'll know before night whether you are really a high-priced man or not.[2]

Taylor's system made sense in the first half of this century, when a firm's competitive advantage came from exploiting economies of scale—assembling standardized products on long assembly lines instead of in small batches. The resulting decline in cost and price created a mass market of consumers who found they could afford a new world of products. Henry Ford's Model T was the paradigm case. Exploiting economies of scale required unprecedented coordination on the assembly line: parts from different places had to reach a worker at precisely the right time. Taylor's insistence on uniform worker actions fitted well with this system. The resulting products lacked variety, but the many consumers who had never owned an automobile or an electric refrigerator or a radio didn't mind.

Over time, mass markets became saturated and the potential for further economies of scale diminished. As incomes rose, consumers became more choosy. Firms began to search for a new competitive advantage. During the 1980s many came to recognize that a reputation for high quality, good service, and frequent product improvement could provide this edge.

To achieve quality, service, and continuous improvement, firms would have to rely much more heavily on their frontline workers for problem solving and ideas. They would have to hire a different kind of frontline worker and manage those workers in ways that fostered their initiative and skills. It is this transformation that underlies both the New Basic Skills and the Five Principles.

How many of the nation's employers are organizing production in this way? On the basis of a 1992 survey, Professor Paul Osterman of M.I.T. estimates that approximately 35 percent of firms with 50 or more employees are doing so, using practices such as quality circles, total quality management, and innovative payment plans.[3] A 1994 survey of employers by the National Center on the Educational Quality of the Workforce found a similar pattern.[4] Surveys of Fortune 1000 firms by Edward Lawler and his colleagues every three years since 1987 show that the percentage of large firms adopting high-performance work organization is growing, and the most recent survey results are consistent with Osterman's.[5] These survey results are also consistent with the economywide patterns reported in Chapter 2: the payoff for mastery of the New Basic Skills is growing, and opportunities for labor force entrants who lack these skills are declining.

What do the Five Principles mean in practice? We can answer the question for business by returning to Honda and Northwestern Mutual Life.

1. ENSURE THAT ALL FRONTLINE WORKERS UNDERSTAND THE PROBLEM.

In Diann Buckner's and Bill Bourbeau's first weeks at Honda of America, they heard again and again: "Accept no bad parts, make no bad parts, pass no bad parts." The message is a central component of the firm's philosophy: quality is not solely the job of inspectors at the end of the production line; it is the responsibility of every worker.

The message is reinforced in the Quality Communications Plaza, centrally located in the Marysville plant. The plaza's walls are covered with summaries of results from customer surveys, quality information from the Vehicle Quality Department, and goals and production figures from all departments. On the plaza floor is a changing display of vehicles made by Honda and other manufacturers. All these displays serve as reminders to associates of the connection between their performance and Honda's market position.

The message is transmitted more actively through "town meetings" held at least once a quarter to inform employees about Honda's market performance and what that performance means for them. During the 1990–1992 recession, part of one town meeting was spent addressing rumors that had spread through the plant concerning layoffs. Employees were asked to write down on note cards what they had heard, and a few days later management distributed responses clarifying the firm's plans.

As a mutual insurance company, NML is owned by its policyholders. It embraces a mission statement, first promulgated in 1888, which begins: "The ambition of the Northwestern has been less to be large than to be safe; its aim is to rank first in benefits to policyowners rather than first in size." The mission is presented to employees as part of a reciprocal compact. NML has honored the compact by avoiding boom-and-bust strategies and so has never been forced to lay off employees, a fact well known in Milwaukee. In return for this corporate commitment, NML emphasizes that its employees must go "the extra mile" to satisfy customers' needs. That message begins in the hiring process (Chapter 2). It continues in the expectation that employees will use the company's opportunities for training and advancement to move up the occupational structure, a structure more hierarchical than Honda's. Monthly newsletters inform employees of the progress of new initiatives, how they relate to the company's goals, and what they mean for employees.

In these ways, each company works hard to explain to its employees what it needs to accomplish to succeed and the relationship between individual performance and corporate success.

2. DESIGN JOBS SO THAT ALL FRONTLINE WORKERS HAVE BOTH INCENTIVES AND OPPORTUNITIES TO CONTRIBUTE TO SOLUTIONS.

HAM has an elaborate system of incentives, the Voluntary Improvement Program (VIP), to encourage workers to engage in a variety of activities that improve quality, reduce cost, and increase safety.

Suggestions

While working at one of her team's jobs on the assembly line, Diann Buckner noticed that an associate was having difficulty shooting a black bolt into a black part. Guessing that the problem was inadequate lighting, she thought that taping a flashlight to the air gun might solve the problem. She followed the established procedure for making suggestions, fill-ing out a one-page form describing her idea. The next day she received approval for the suggestion and was told to try it out. After some experimenting, she found a way to attach the flashlight that solved the problem. Buckner then described her solution on the back of the one-page form and submitted it for review. For her suggestion she received a small cash bonus and VIP points, which accumulate toward significant financial rewards. Solving the lighting problem illustrates both the skills Diann brought to Honda—literacy, initiative, problem solving, ability to communicate—and the firm's success in fostering the use of these skills.

Like Diann Buckner's suggestion, most of the 12,000 suggestions submitted each year are for small changes. HAM management is convinced that quality improvements and cost reductions come from continuous implementation of a great many ideas for small, but meaningful changes provided by associates. For this reason, it approves approximately 70 percent of the suggestions submitted by associates and provides the resources needed to implement them.

NH Circles

Each New Honda (NH) Circle consists of a small group of associates who identify a problem and want to work to solve it. The problem may concern quality, cost, or safety. After management has approved an NH Circle project (approximately 95 percent are approved), the circle members may work one hour per week of overtime on their project. In addition, group members are encouraged to participate in an eight-hour training session that teaches them about quality-control tools useful in carrying out circle activities. The tools include checksheets, bar graphs, line graphs, area graphs, cause-and-effect diagrams, and Pareto diagrams—all of which the Sharpshooters used in solving the stopped-blower-nut problem.

When an NH Circle has completed its work, the group must make a presentation lasting no more than 18 minutes to a panel of the department's managers, showing what problem it addressed, what procedures it used to tackle the problem, what solution was found, and what evidence was collected and analyzed to verify the value of the solution. The presentation typically includes visual displays such as Figures 3.1 and 3.2. The best presentations are entered in a plant-level competition, and the plant-level winners go on to a North American competition.

After the presentation to management has been made, each circle member receives $15 and 50 VIP points. In 1985, the year in which HAM started quality circles, there were 14 registered circles. Today there are more than 300 active circles at Honda of America.

Each associate accumulates VIP points as a result of implementing suggestions or participating in an NH Circle. A total of 1,000 VIP points results in a Silver Award of $800. When the total reaches 2,500 points, the associate receives a Gold Award of a Honda Civic automobile or a Honda Goldwing motorcycle. A cumulative total of 5,000 points results in a Honda Award, entitling the associate to a Honda Accord, two coach airfare tickets to anywhere in the world, two extra weeks of vacation with pay, and spending money equal to four weeks of base pay. (The Honda Award has a value of approximately $28,500.) Four Honda Awards have been earned since the program was started in 1985.

At Honda of America the awards for individual suggestions are small; the big payoff comes from accumulation.
The message is clear: it is sustained initiative over an
extended period of time that receives the greatest rewards.

The core of NML's strategy for promoting initiative is a
policy of promotion from within. Mary Grace James first
went to work at NML as a co-op student in 1982, when she
was a junior in high school. After graduation she went to
work full-time for NML as a messenger. From messenger she
moved to the mail desk; then to typing policy change information on a computer; then to service assistant, a secretarial
position answering phones and taking messages. In 1991,
she applied for and was chosen for a position as a disabilities analyst. After eight months, she became a senior disability benefits analyst. In this position, James reviews policyholders' claims for disability payments. Her typical day
involves time on the phone with clients and co-workers, time
on the computer, and time analyzing claim-relevant records.
She can, without the review of more senior staff, award payments of up to $3,000 per month.

Karen Pawlak and Mary Grace James are only two of a
great many employees who started working at NML as secretaries or messengers and who over time, through a combination of skills, initiative, and training, moved to positions
requiring significant skills and paying attractive salaries.
This policy provides strong incentives for workers to display
initiative and to invest in learning skills that are valuable to
the firm.

NML's practice of promotion from within also helps to
explain why the firm devotes considerable resources to
screening applicants for entry-level positions, even though

most such positions do not require mastery of the New Basic Skills. As one NML manager commented, "I consider it a failure if a person hired for an entry-level position is still in that job 18 months later."

3. PROVIDE ALL FRONTLINE WORKERS WITH THE TRAINING NEEDED TO PURSUE SOLUTIONS EFFECTIVELY.

Diann Buckner and Bill Bourbeau began training during their first day at HAM. But, as is the case with most HAM associates, their participation in training did not end with the two weeks involved in learning how to do their first assembly job. They are among the 80 percent of HAM associates who have taken part in training during the past year.

Two aspects of HAM training programs are striking. First, they are closely linked to the company's philosophy of empowering workers to collaborate in identifying and solving problems. Titles of the programs include "Principles for Problem Solving," "Better Communications," and "Unstressed for Success." Similarly, many of the training programs for team leaders are aimed at developing facilitation skills. As one trainer put it, "A leader must be a facilitator rather than a doer."

The second striking characteristic of the training programs is the extent to which their design promotes change in behavior. The firm recognizes that only if there are behavior changes can investments in training pay off. For this reason, every training program has extensive follow-up to assure that training leads to changes in how associates do their jobs. The tight connection between training and job behavior seems self-evident, but, as we explain in Chapter 6, it is missing from many professional development programs aimed at improving the effectiveness of teachers.

According to Karen Pawlak, "As an underwriter [at NML] you are always in training." In 1990 she completed four months of full-time training before starting with a small case load, which slowly increased in size and complexity as she gained skill. During the past year Pawlak has spent 30 hours in training learning about advances in medical treatments and new techniques for analyzing applicants' finances.

All of Mary Grace James's new jobs have also involved training, which became more intensive as the jobs advanced. Her first six months as a disabilities benefits analyst were spent largely in training. For 10 weeks the trainer took the novice analysts through increasingly complex cases, discussing what evidence to collect and how to evaluate it. James was then given a small case load, and training continued for another 14 weeks at a less intensive pace, with an emphasis on how to deal with more difficult cases, such as those dealing with claims for partial disability.

The amount of time Pawlak and James have spent in training is typical. Each year more than half of home office employees participate in formal training programs offered by the Human Resources Division. In addition, each division that provides services to clients has its own training programs.

One emphasis in the training conducted by the Human Resources Division is communication skills as the titles of its workshops make clear: Building High-Achieving Teams, Interpersonal Managing Skills, Persuasive Writing, Speaking with Impact, Working: Resolving Issues with Others. This emphasis is also apparent in the titles of many self-study programs offered by the division: Dealing with Difficult Behavior, How to Teach Grown-ups, Team Building.

Training at NML is closely connected to the work of the firm and to the problems managers perceive as hindering productivity. As at Honda, training must lead to changes in the way employees do their jobs or it isn't worth pursuing.

4. MEASURE PROGRESS ON A REGULAR BASIS.

In the automobile industry there are many signals of how well a firm is faring. Market shares are published quarterly in the *Wall Street Journal*, J. D. Power surveys of consumer satisfaction are published in major newspapers every year. Each April *Consumer Reports* publishes detailed comparative information on defect and safety records. Management cannot fail to be aware of how well its company's products are faring relative to the competition.

HAM does not wait for media reports to provide feedback on the firm's success. It monitors operations closely, checking continually that goals for costs and defect rates are on target and that training investments are resulting in payoffs. Much of this information is displayed on computer monitors located throughout the plant and on the walls of the Quality Communications Plaza.

One of NML's most innovative means of measuring progress toward organizational goals is the Policyowners' Examining Committee. Each year since 1907 the firm's board of trustees has selected three to five prominent policy owners—usually with business experience—to serve on this committee. The committee's mandate is to evaluate the performance of NML's policies, operations, and management and to make recommendations to the trustees about how the firm's performance could be improved. Each year the committee decides which aspects of the company's policies to examine in detail, and all the company's records and personnel are at its disposal. The reports of this committee provide NML's management with an outside view of whether its practices are consistent with emerging market conditions and changing technology. Its recommendations have led to changes such as the establishment of a Controller's Department, a more formal corporate planning process, and greater emphasis on economic forecasting.

NML also has a variety of internal strategies for monitoring its performance. It pays close attention to market share. It regularly compares the cost of its policies with those of competitors. It keeps close track of the percentage of telephone queries that are answered by the person initially handling the inquiry and the length of time it takes to process claims on policies and applications for new policies. Finally, it pays close attention to the satisfaction level and concerns of the hundreds of independent insurance agents who sell its policies. All these monitoring efforts are designed to prevent isolation from customers and employees.

5. PERSEVERE AND LEARN FROM MISTAKES; THERE ARE NO MAGIC BULLETS.

The Sharpshooters did not solve the stopped-blower-nut problem on the first try, or the second, or the third. It took eight months and six proposals to lick the problem. Management did not give up on the Sharpshooters after the first two proposals failed to solve the problem.

Honda of America management also makes mistakes.

One Wednesday in October, HAM management announced scheduled overtime for a Saturday in November, a fairly common occurrence during a year of high sales. This time the announcement led to uncharacteristic widespread grumbling on the shop floor. That Saturday was the date of the Ohio State–Michigan football game, an important event to many Honda associates. By the end of the week, management recognized the mistake and rescheduled the overtime for another Saturday.

At NML as at Honda of America, mistakes are made and unexpected problems arise. In an attempt to answer all client phone calls promptly, all six customer representatives in a policyowners' services group were told to answer calls at the same time. While this strategy provided quick initial responses, it also left the customer reps with no time to research customer questions. The customer service representatives discussed their frustration with this arrangement and proposed an alternative: at any one time three representatives would answer the phone while the other three followed up on customer questions and wrote the necessary letters. Management approved, and the new arrangement was introduced.

A more critical example of the importance of persistence at NML is the implementation of Workbench. Its introduction was characterized by numerous unexpected delays and frustrations; it took seven years before all underwriters were using the system. NML management learned from the delays and setbacks, and persevered.

LESSONS FROM BEST-PRACTICE FIRMS

Honda of America and Northwestern Mutual Life are two well-managed firms that have provided good jobs for many years. Underlying their management practices is the basic assumption that workers acquire knowledge on the job that is critical to improving the performance of the organization. Creating opportunities and incentives for workers to bring this knowledge to bear on organizational problems is a powerful strategy for fostering productivity growth. Although the actual management practices and corporate cultures of the two firms differ in many respects, the policies of both reflect the same five underlying principles. These principles, *used together*, offer guidelines for improving the performance of a wide range of organizations, including public schools.

The relevance of the Five Principles for improving schooling does not assume that schools are just like firms; as we saw in Chapter 1, schools differ from firms in the array of frontline workers and the extent of freedom of action. Nor does the relevance assume that firms always get things right. To the contrary, the Five Principles grew out of a realization by thoughtful managers that they were getting it wrong, that the single-minded pursuit of economies of scale no longer provided competitive advantage. Even among successful firms, getting it wrong is part of a natural cycle: a firm prospers by exploiting a successful strategy; but success leads the firm to hold blindly to its strategy while the market changes, and the strategy begins to fail. Recognizing failure and the need for change is a slow and painful process.

Return for a moment to the story of the Ford Model T (Chapter 1). In 1921, the Model T had given Ford Motor Company an enormous market advantage. By 1926, the advantage had been squandered. Ford could argue that the 1926 Model T was a better car than its 1921 cousin—and it would be right. In each year, Ford had improved the Model T in a number of small ways. The problem was that the competition was improving much faster and the Model T's small improvements left it further and further behind in the market.

Today's schools look much like Ford in 1926. The products they produce—student achievement levels—are not worse than they were 20 years ago; in most respects they are slightly better. But in those 20 years, the job market has changed radically. Just as the Model T that was good enough in 1921 was not good enough in 1926, the education that was adequate for high-wage employers in 1970 is no longer adequate today. Only recovery strategies that embody the Five Principles can get to the heart of the problem. Effective change requires fostering the performance of all frontline workers—in the case of schools, the teachers, the students, and the parents.

To see why this is so, consider the discordance between the Five Principles and current school practice:

1. Ensure that all frontline workers understand the problem.

A critical goal for every school must be preparing students for today's and tomorrow's good jobs. But many teachers, parents, and students still do not recognize how fast skill requirements for good jobs have increased in the last decade, and schools have failed to keep up with those changes.

2. Design jobs so that all frontline workers have both incentives and opportunities to contribute to solutions.

Most students see little connection between what they are learning and future job prospects and so have little incentive to work hard. Few teachers have opportunities or incentives to learn about the changing job market or to change their teaching methods so that they focus on the New Basic Skills. Few parents have opportunities and incentives to collaborate with teachers to improve their children's education.

3. Provide all frontline workers with the training needed to pursue solutions effectively.

Today, most teachers have access to two kinds of professional development: one-day workshops with no follow-up, and graduate courses offered at colleges and universities. Neither has been very effective in promoting the teaching of the New Basic Skills. Most parents have even fewer opportunities to learn how to help their children acquire the New Basic Skills.

4. Measure progress on a regular basis.

In most schools, student achievement is measured through tests that place a premium on one kind of learning: the memorization of facts. Such tests ignore many of the New Basic Skills: the ability to structure problems and to test solutions, the ability to write clear English, the ability to work constructively in groups.

5. Persevere and learn from mistakes; there are no magic bullets.

Current debate over school reform centers on magic bullets: more money, school choice, charter schools, and national standards. Each proposal is promoted as a complete solution to the educational problem, yet each, if it works, is only a first step, an impetus for change. The dirty work of change—exactly what is to be changed, who will do the changing, and which pieces come first—is never mentioned. When people fail to confront these questions, they are not focusing on what matters. The problems that inevitably accompany change look to them like failure, so they give up.

The Five Principles grew out of a need to improve quality and productivity. But best-practice firms are not the only organizations that have embraced these principles. Across the nation, a small group of schools have developed their own versions of the Five Principles to teach students the New Basic Skills. All of these schools (or groups of schools) ultimately embraced all of the Five Principles. Each of the schools began by emphasizing one of the principles: understanding the problem in one case, improving training in another.

The following chapters tell the stories of these schools—one chapter for each principle. These stories are about works in progress. None is a story of instant success. But for those who would see schools prepare students for tomorrow's economy, the chapters show how to proceed.

CHAPTER 4

THE FIRST PRINCIPLE
AGREE ON THE PROBLEM

THE ESSENTIAL ROLE OF PARENTS

The world is full of challenging problems: eliminating stopped blower nuts, implementing the Underwriters' Workbench, getting a sixth-grade girl or boy to turn off the television and do homework. Neither presidents nor principals can solve the problems by themselves. Solving each problem requires the initiative and skills of all frontline workers, the persons closest to the situation. In the case of homework, frontline workers include parents. But parents can't help to solve a problem they don't know exists.

T. A. Vasquez and her husband, Albert, live around the corner from the Zavala Elementary School in East Austin, Texas. Austin has a reputation for good public schools, but the reputation comes from other parts of the city. Zavala serves poor children. The average family income is $12,000, and until recently the school's academic reputation was weak. All four of T. A. and Albert's children have gone to Zavala. Their three oldest children got good grades, but none was advised to enter the college-prep track in high school. The Vasquezes found this puzzling. Now their youngest daughter, Dorothy, was getting A's and B's in the first grade and seemed to face a similarly puzzling future.

The missing link was test scores. T. A. and Albert did not know that their older children all scored in the bottom quartile on the Texas Assessment of Academic Skills (TAAS), the set of standardized tests taken by all children in Texas public schools. None of Zavala's teachers took it upon themselves to tell T. A. and Albert about these scores. The Vasquez children were scoring no lower than other children at Zavala. Besides, what could be expected of children from poor families in which few many parents spoke English or seemed to care about schooling?

The absence of parental involvement with their children's academic skills extends beyond the poor neighborhoods of East Austin. Similar stories can be told about schools in every state. Consider again three facts presented in Chapters 1 and 2.

- In 1979, 30-year-old men with a high school diploma earned a yearly average of $27,500 (in 1993 dollars). By 1993, 30-year-old men with a high school diploma earned a yearly average of $20,000.
- In 1992, the math and reading test scores of half of all 17-year-olds across the nation were too low to get a job in a modern automobile plant.
- In 1995, 65 percent of U.S. parents gave their oldest child's school a grade of A or B, an approval rating that has remained relatively unchanged since the Gallup pollsters began asking this question in 1985. More probing questions detected parental concerns about educational quality, but awareness of a skills problem was only beginning to emerge.[1]

Parents care deeply about their children's future. Their

misplaced confidence in their children's education reflects out-of-date experience. In the 1970s, when most parents of today's high school students were coming of age, a high school diploma was still a ticket to the U.S. middle class. Many parents have failed to see the subsequent rise in skill requirements for a good job. Other parents have seen the rise but only as an indication of a need to attend college. Few parents have seen it for what it is: an urgent signal of the need to teach a set of New Basic Skills from kindergarten through twelfth grade.

Until very recently, this out-of-date knowledge has gone along with a paralyzing explanation for low U.S. skills. Why do children in Asia know so much more math and science than children in the United States? U.S. parents attributed the achievement gap to differences in ability rather than differences in student effort. By contrast, Asian parents believe that effort is the more important factor. Attitudes toward learning translate into attitudes toward schools. Asian parents are relatively dissatisfied with their schools. They believe, despite their children's achievement, that their schools should require more hard work. U.S. parents were generally satisfied with their schools, in part because they believe that making students work harder would not produce much learning.[2]

In the most recent poll data, this explanation—an excuse, really—is beginning to dissolve. A Public Agenda poll conducted in the summer of 1995 indicates that three times as many parents now believe that good grades come more from hard work than from being born with strong intellectual abilities.[3] The trick is to translate these attitude shifts into action.

It is not an easy trick to accomplish. Even among parents

who see the need for higher skills, many feel powerless to change the schools. These parents have a mirror image in the many teachers who begin careers resolving to teach effectively, to make a difference in their students' lives. Over time, they retreat because they recognize that schools cannot teach more rigorous skills without strong parental support, support for the idea that mastery of the New Basic Skills is more important than winning sports teams and important enough to turn off the television to do homework.

The details of energizing parents and teachers vary from one school to the next. But recounting the story of one school that is struggling to change shows what is involved: how long it takes, the inevitable false starts, the need for outside help—not to do things for parents and teachers, but to help them to learn how to do things for themselves. The story of Zavala Elementary School in East Austin, Texas, illustrates what it means to Agree on the Problem.

THE ZAVALA ELEMENTARY SCHOOL IN 1991

Twenty years ago, Austin was known as the capital of Texas and the home of the University of Texas Longhorns. Today Austin is also home to Dell Computer and many other high-tech firms. With the university and the high-tech firms come many well-educated parents who understand the importance of skills.

Most of the high tech rings the perimeter of the city; Zavala Elementary School is located in the core of East Austin. The original building and 18 portable classrooms sit on Robert Martinez Jr. Street between Santa Rita Courts and Chalmers Courts, two public housing projects. For 60 percent of the Zavala families, Spanish is the first language.

In 1991 the percentage of Zavala students who passed the state-mandated TAAS tests was about half the district average. Among Austin's 63 elementary schools, Zavala ranked thirty-third in school attendance. It was a school where most teachers did not want to be. At year's end, 16 of Zavala's 38 teachers left for other jobs.

T. A. Vasquez, Anna Aquino, Lourdes Zamarron, and Rachel Gonzalez had watched their older children go through Zavala. They were disappointed when their children not admitted to middle-school magnet programs, but they were not sure of the cause because their children's grades had been good. They knew it was not a good sign that teachers didn't stay long at Zavala, but they did not know the reasons. As Lourdes Zamarron asked, "Why don't these teachers want to stay here and teach my child?" T. A. Vasquez recalled parents' attitudes in previous years: "I could walk in here on a PTA night and there'd be maybe five, ten parents here . . . parents didn't have an inkling of what was going on at the school, how their kids were being taught."

Zavala's problem was not a lack of money. As part of the settlement of a school desegregation suit, the Austin school district had designated Zavala and 15 other low-achieving, minority elementary schools as "priority schools." Beginning in 1987, the 16 priority schools had received an additional $300,000 per year—enough money to make a difference.

Nor was Zavala's problem an indifferent principal. Todd McDowell, a science teacher who had been at Zavala six years, said: "You would've thought [the principal] was a strong leader. He spent a lot of time [at Zavala], he worked real hard. But it was subtle the things he didn't do, and the things he didn't do were some of the things that we needed."

Samantha Bednarski, a young first-grade teacher in her fourth year at Zavala, viewed the principal similarly: "a real nice, easygoing principal . . . very concerned about the Hispanic community. [He] tried to do some different things, but he didn't get a lot of support."

Change had to come to Zavala from the outside.

THE TEXAS INDUSTRIAL AREAS FOUNDATION

Short, stout, with long gray hair and a briefcase full of new books to read, Ernesto Cortes loves ideas and loves to argue. He has spent his adult life finding ways to help the poor to help themselves. After graduating from Texas A&M, Cortes worked in Chicago under the radical community organizer Saul Alinsky. He then returned to Texas in 1974 to head the Texas Industrial Areas Foundation (TIAF), an organization committed to helping poor families to gain the power to improve their lives.

From the beginning, TIAF followed the Iron Rule that Alinsky had preached: Never do for others what they can do for themselves. A TIAF organizer, supported by local churches, would begin by identifying issues of common concern—the lack of paved streets, the need for sewers. Next the organizer would identify neighborhood leaders and help the community to build organizations with the political power to get the problems fixed. In this work, the dusty streets of East Austin were like the offices of NML and the Honda factory floor. In each place, progress depended on broad-scale participation, and participation required broad-scale agreement on the nature of the problem.

When TIAF organizers had focused on schools, they had

organized around passing bond issues to get more money for schools serving poor children. They reasoned that lack of money was a major obstacle to better schools and that a combination of teachers who loved kids and the smaller classes money could buy would lead to higher achievement. Their greatest victory of their first decade was the passage of Texas House Bill 72, in which the state legislature authorized more than $1 billion in additional funding for schools, much of which would go to schools serving poor children.

During the late 1980s, events led Cortes and the TIAF community organizers to rethink their approach. The collapse of the Texas oil industry reduced state tax revenues and led to underfunding of the school aid authorized by HB 72. With less money, TIAF's goal of better schools through smaller class size became increasingly less viable. TIAF also saw that few of the schools that had received extra money under HB 72 had shown consistent gains in student achievement.

The basis of a different approach came from Allied Communities of Tarrant (ACT), the TIAF group in Fort Worth. In the early 1980s, ACT had achieved remarkable success in transforming Morningside Middle School, a low-income, minority school with low achievement scores. ACT had focused on building a Morningside parent organization that could demand change and could work with teachers to change the school's culture. During ACT's first four years at Morningside, students' average achievement scores rose from last among the district's 20 middle schools to third.[4]

ACT's success at Morningside, shrinking funds, and the realization that money alone did not always create good schools led Cortes and the TIAF organizers to develop a school improvement strategy that focused on building "communities of learners." The strategy would have three components:

Getting parents to recognize that low achievement is the problem

Getting parents in a position to participate in school governance

Getting the extra money, where needed, to provide a quality education

Parent-teacher-administrator teams with greater autonomy concerning use of resources would play a key role in bringing about change. But school-based management was not to be an end in itself: its purpose was to create the incentives and opportunities for frontline workers—teachers and parents and students—to make and carry out decisions that would result in greater student achievement.

Ernie Cortes knew that a community would adopt this strategy more readily if it knew others were using it too. He sought to build a network of schools working to change with TIAF assistance. In 1992 he convinced Skip Meno, the recently appointed state commissioner of education, to commit the state department of education to join with TIAF to form the Alliance Schools Network, whose members would include parents and teachers working with TIAF organizers to improve individual schools. Starting with 32 schools, the Alliance has grown to more than 60.

These numbers, displayed on a chart, would make a bright picture of success. Behind the picture would be hours of gritty one-on-one work. NML, Honda, and Diamond-Star screen for workers who agree that quality improvement is their problem. The average U.S. school can't screen for its parents. It has to work with those it has—men and women, half of whom have not gone beyond high school, many of whom are uncertain that weak skills are a problem. More often than not, they lack the language to lobby schools to raise their standards.

AN INITIAL SETBACK

In 1990 Austin Interfaith, TIAF's group in Austin, chose its first school project. Blackshear Elementary was a poor, largely black school located close to two of the churches supporting Austin Interfaith's work. The project began with a mistake. Before choosing Blackshear, Interfaith had talked to Blackshear's principal, but only on a superficial level. They had offered to help with "parental involvement." The principal had agreed. Little more was said.

Interfaith's lead organizer was Joe Higgs, young, softspoken, polite to all, and dogged. He spent a year trying to organize Blackshear's parents to participate in their children's education. Nothing happened. The obstacle was the principal. To the principal parental involvement meant that parents would come to PTA meetings and take greater responsibility for their children's behavior and homework. Parental involvement did not mean discussing changes in the curriculum or how it was taught. With these issues off the table, it was hard to get Blackshear parents interested, and education could not improve.

After a year, Interfaith gave up on Blackshear. It had learned a sobering, but valuable lesson: agreement on the problem meant just that—agreement by *all* participants.

Organizing parents around achievement would be impossible unless the school leadership was committed to change.

CRISIS AT ZAVALA

In December 1990, the Zavala principal resigned. The school board appointed as acting principal Alejandro Mindiz-Melton, Zavala's assistant principal for the previous five years. When he was appointed, Al Melton's résumé provided few clues that in three years he would appear on "Good Morning America" as one of three "Heroes in American Education" chosen by the Reader's Digest Foundation.

Melton was born in Youngsport, Texas, a ranching community 60 miles north of Austin. Because of his father's career in the military, his family moved often and he attended public schools in many parts of the country. After two years at Santa Monica College in California, he completed his bachelor's degree with a major in science education at the University of Texas, earning extra money by working part-time as a teacher's assistant. He taught for three years in Killeen, Texas, and moved to the Austin schools in 1981.

A stocky, informal man of medium height, Melton was popular with Zavala parents even though he had not grown up speaking Spanish. He quickly learned the names of students and parents and worked hard to improve his Spanish. Unlike his predecessor, Al Melton realized that improving education at Zavala required many changes. In his words, "The staff was dispirited, and there was low achievement, had been for a long time. We needed to really change, and we had not been honest with the community or ourselves about student performance. Huge percentages of students were on the honor roll. You know, most kids were taking home A's and B's on their report cards. We were not accurately reporting student progress to parents. There was grade inflation."

One of the first things Al Melton did was to ask a parent, Albert Soto, to read aloud at a PTA meeting the achievement test scores of Zavala's students. When Soto realized how low Zavala children were scoring, he became enraged and accused the teachers of failing to educate his children and other children in the community.

It was the start of a bumpy ride. Soto immediately withdrew his three children from Zavala. Other parents were upset. Teachers were angry and hurt. Claudia Santamaria, a young bilingual education teacher in her second year at Zavala at the time, described the teachers' response to Mr. Soto.

> Mr. Soto pretty much ran the meeting. He kept talking about the TAAS tests. . . . [He said], "These people are telling us that our children can't learn."
> The teachers were sinking in their seats. This had never been said. . . . The parents started talking out. It was hard; a lot of the teachers were almost crying, especially the teachers who had been at Zavala for a long time. We felt it was an attack on us. Mr. Soto said that the best teachers must be at other schools. We wanted Mr. Melton to get up to defend us, and it did not happen.
> The meeting was about an hour. . . . It was depressing, man.

Al Melton's beginning left Joe Higgs and Austin Interfaith with a tough decision. Unlike the principal at Blackshear, Melton was committed to change at Zavala. But his first steps had demoralized teachers and worsened relationships between teachers and parents. Melton was willing to lead, but Higgs was uncertain that Zavala would hold together long enough for parents to participate. Ultimately, Higgs was impressed by Melton's enthusiasm and his willingness to stake his reputation on improving Zavala's education. He asked if Melton would support Interfaith's efforts to organize Zavala parents. Melton invited Higgs and Kathleen Davis, a lawyer with grown children who had recently joined the Interfaith staff, to begin talking with Zavala's parents and teachers. They reached an agreement that later in the year the faculty would vote on whether to establish a formal relationship with Austin Interfaith.

Higgs, who spoke Spanish well, spent the fall of 1991 meeting with individual Zavala parents. He was following TIAF's first and second steps: Find issues that many parents care about, and find potential leaders among the parents. In numerous conversations, he asked parents:

Why didn't they attend PTA meetings? (The most common answer: they were useless.)
What did they want from the school? (They were surprised to be asked.)
What were their greatest needs? (They had many, but found it difficult initially to articulate them.)

Joe Higgs's meetings sound like baby steps. But this is where we are as a nation. Schools can't get better unless parents want them to get better and know how to participate in making them better. Higgs and his co-workers understood this. They knew there were no quick fixes in developing parental commitment for the changes needed to give every child the skills to get a good job.

ZAVALA GETS HEALTHY

By the end of the fall of 1991, Joe Higgs and Kathleen Davis had come to know several women who cared deeply about what happened to their children at Zavala and seemed interested in helping to organize other parents. T. A. Vasquez was one of these women. Rachel Gonzalez, Anna Aquino, and Lourdes Zamarron were others.

The meetings also helped to identify three issues of concern to a great many Zavala parents. The first was inadequate health care: their children were often ill, and there was a two-month waiting period for an appointment at the nearest city health clinic eight blocks away. The second concern was neighborhood security and crime: the housing projects in which the majority of Zavala families lived were infested with drug dealers, and theft and violence were all too common a part of daily life. The third concern was the lack of jobs and constructive activities for teenagers and the consequent significance of gangs in their lives. Parents cared about achievement in a general way; some had heard about Albert Soto's meeting. But Zavala was one of the schools described at the end of Chapter 1 in which education could improve only if other problems were addressed as well.

During the first half of the 1991–92 school year, Joe Higgs also met individually with Claudia Santamaria, Todd McDowell, and the other Zavala teachers to ask them about their concerns. The teachers, remembering Mr. Soto's outrage, emphasized the low achievement of Zavala children.

When asked why it was so low, they often mentioned the children's poor health: 35 percent had not received all of the state-required immunizations; 14 percent had untreated hearing or vision problems. Poor health, the teachers felt, contributed to poor attendance.

In the early spring of 1992, the Zavala teachers, with the support of the principal, voted to enter a formal relationship with Austin Interfaith aimed at improving the lives of Zavala's children. For Al Melton, it was not a difficult decision:

> I'm not exactly sure how [Austin Interfaith] came here. Someone sent them, I don't know who, maybe God, because they were a godsend as far as I'm concerned. . . . What I liked about them was they were not talking about a new program or a new system or a new curriculum, but they were really talking about systemic change in the community, and that's really where, I felt, the change had to come from. The community had to change for the school to be successful. And they talked about organizing parents to be involved in the governance of schools, and I found that very attractive, and so we entered into a partnership. It's the wisest decision this faculty ever made. We spent many months discussing it.

For some of Zavala's teachers the decision was not so easy. Claudia Santamaria described the teachers' questions and fears:

> I think it was a lack of knowledge on our part. Who were they? What did they want? What was in it for them?
>
> Austin Interfaith was so political, and teachers are not political; they tend to be subservient, flexible, nurturing. . . . [Austin Interfaith] would ask, "What's bad about East Austin? What's good about East Austin?" and this [questioning] intimidated some teachers; it made a lot of waves.

What if we get fired? What if we get in trouble? It is easier just to go with the flow. . . .

It took a lot of talking among the staff. It took a lot of asking ourselves where we wanted to go; where we were. . . . The expectations were so low. Austin Interfaith turned this around. There were eight or nine of us that had only been at Zavala for one or two years and we were more accepting. . . . The few teachers who were really against Austin Interfaith—they are gone.

By the spring of 1992, Higgs and T. A. Vasquez and the other potential parent leaders had compiled a short list of issues. First on the list was the health of the children, something important to parents and teachers alike. Their next step was to organize a walk through the neighborhood to develop broader support.

On a warm sunny Saturday morning in May, 20 teams consisting of Zavala teachers, the potential parent leaders, and members of congregations supporting Austin Interfaith knocked on the door of every apartment and house in the neighborhood. At each door, they requested a few minutes to explain the agenda for change. The walk conveyed information but it also began to heal the rift between parents and teachers. As Samantha Bednarski, a young first-grade teacher, put it: "It was really neat as a teacher because when you're walking through the projects, all the kids see you and recognize you and they think it's neat that you want to go to where they live, and even the little ones are saying hi . . . most of the people who were home were very open to us . . . they might have wondered why we were there, but I think, deep inside, it kind of made them probably feel important . . . that we were coming to their house and wanting to know their opinions."

As T. A. Vasquez saw the walks:

> That's where it started, just by talking to each other. . . .
> The parents talking with the teachers, the teachers willing
> to get out of [the school] and going out to the parents'
> homes and visiting with them for five or 10 minutes in the
> house. And when the teachers came back from a lot of
> those walks, they were saying, "You know, a lot of these
> parents, some of their homes are so poor, yet they invited us
> into their houses, they wanted to know if we wanted a
> Coke or coffee, a donut, a taco, and you could tell they did-
> n't have much, and that made a big impression on the
> teachers because some of these teachers, the majority of
> these teachers, all they did was just come to the building
> and go back home. . . . They were doing their work, . . . but
> they didn't really relate to the people outside until they
> started going on these walks, and it kind of opened up a lot
> of things with the parents starting to feel more comfortable
> with the teachers, and the teachers likewise.

Building on the walk's momentum, Higgs and Davis
began to organize a Rally for Zavala to formalize the partnership among parents and teachers. The rally was built
around the goals developed in the fall: improved health care
for Zavala children, better neighborhood security, jobs for
teenagers, and improved student achievement. Three hundred people attended the rally, including Austin's mayor, the
school board president, the superintendent, and the head of
Austin's health department. Only 50 of the people were
Zavala parents, most of whom still believed that nothing
would change. Most people at the rally were representatives
of the 25 congregations supporting Austin Interfaith.

The Rally for Zavala failed to energize parents but it
made progress on the issue of health: the mayor committed

the city government to bring the immunizations of all Zavala children up to date. He also formalized the goals of the partnership.

After the rally the Interfaith organizers and the more interested parents continued to work on the rally's four goals. They focused first on security in the housing projects. Higgs, Davis, and Lourdes Zamarron, a Zavala parent, got the Austin police drug task force to target the two housing projects serving Zavala families for several weeks. They discussed with the director of Austin's housing the possibility of identifying the apartments out of which drugs were sold openly. But as the summer progressed it became clear that however disturbed the residents were by drug selling, they were too scared to identify dealers.

Recall that the last of the Five Principles is perseverance. Perseverance seems obvious but it requires constant reinforcement. In August 1992, Austin Interfaith's attempt to create a Community of Learners was like NML's Underwriters' Workbench in 1990—a good idea that was two years old and had borne very little fruit. Earlier, Interfaith had tried to organize Blackshear Elementary and had given up. Now, after a year at Zavala, it had only one concrete gain: a mayor's promise to bring immunizations up to date. There were other less tangible gains: a growing trust between teachers and some parents. But without perseverance—without a deep sense of how long things can take—Joe Higgs and Kathleen Davis could have given up and quit.

Rather than quit, the Interfaith organizers returned to the issue of health and the mayor's promise. Again they encountered an obstacle: during the summer, the Austin health department announced that it could not fulfill the mayor's commitment on immunizations because the health clinic nearest to Zavala needed to be closed for removal of asbestos and mold. The organizers then asked: Why couldn't health services be provided at Zavala? After considerable discussion the health department agreed that this was possible, if approved by the school board.

Parents were afraid to finger drug dealers, but they were willing to turn out for health care at Zavala. In October, 200 parents came to a meeting to discuss strategies for obtaining the school board's permission for a clinic. Teachers also came to the meting, and for the first time many parents and teachers saw one another working for the same concrete goal. After meeting individually with school board members and explaining their proposal, the Zavala partnership got the health services proposal on the agenda for the November school board meeting. Parents and teachers began preparations for making the case to the school board.

But the school board grew cautious. Earlier, the board had appointed a task force to develop a sex education curriculum for the public schools. Some members of this task force argued that the introduction of school-based health services would lead to condom distribution and abortion counseling. Anxious to avoid confrontation on a highly charged issue, the school board postponed action on the Zavala clinic until the December meeting.

Attending Austin school board meetings was something new for most Zavala parents. The meetings are held across town in the school district's central offices—the White Castle, as T. A. Vasquez calls it. Meetings begin at 7:30 P.M. and tend to run into the early hours of the morning. For a Zavala parent, attending a meeting means arranging for baby sitting, a fairly long bus ride, and losing much of a night's sleep. Despite these obstacles, 60 Zavala parents came to the December 8 meeting and four delivered short speeches advocating health services at Zavala. Twenty Zavala teachers came as well.

In a series of three-minute talks, the four Zavala parents explained why it was important to have health services at Zavala. Anna Aquino spoke "about my children and how I was caught in between the system. I was not on welfare, so I did not have Medicaid and I was a single parent and . . . couldn't afford health care."

To address condoms and abortion counseling, Sister Theresa, a physically imposing, 65-year-old nun, came to the podium. She told the school board that she knew Zavala families well after working with them for 15 years. They did have a great need for health care services at the school, she said. What the parents wanted were immunizations and care for hearing and vision problems. They did not want, nor would they accept, condom distribution or abortion counseling. She read a letter from the pastor of the Christ Rey Church, located a block from Zavala, emphasizing his support for health services at Zavala. Resistance evaporated. By a unanimous vote, the school board approved health services for Zavala.

WHAT ABOUT EVERYPLACE ELSE?

By this point, the Zavala story raises an obvious question: What about the more than 80,000 schools that don't have Joe Higgs? What are the parents in these schools supposed to do?

Fortunately, the question has an answer. Joe Higgs, good as he is, is not unique. At various schools around the country, organizations are building parental involvement just as Austin Interfaith was doing.

Working in a small basement office in Somerville, Massachusetts, furnished with 40-year-old desks and chairs and several phones, Dan Rothstein, Ana Rodriguez, Luz Santana, and Krystal Robinson design workshops that help low-income parents become advocates for their children's education. The Right Question Project (RQP), like Austin Interfaith, begins from the premise that low-income parents care deeply about their children's education, but do not know how to monitor quality or push for improvement. As Ana Rodriguez commented, "Many parents, especially immigrant parents, have no clue about how the system works. They don't even know whether they can ask questions of teachers."

Unlike most attempts to involve parents with schools, the Right Question Project does not provide parents with information. Instead the workshops focus on helping parents to ask and make use of the answers to questions like "What is my child learning?" "What does my child need to learn?" "Is the teacher teaching what my child needs to learn?" "Is my child learning what he/she needs to learn?" "If the teacher is teaching what my child needs to learn, what else can I do?" "If the teacher is not teaching what my child needs to learn, what do I do?" Recognizing that parents can learn these techniques only if they have seen them practiced, the workshops, facilitated by parents, teachers, or community organizers trained by the RQP staff, use simulations, role playing, and discussion to convey the message.

In a workshop on tracking, the facilitator gives some parents a packet that includes a sheet stating: "The full curriculum is 100 pages long. Your child will be taught the entire 100 pages." Other parents receive a packet with a sheet stating: "The full curriculum is 100 pages long. Your child will be taught only the first 50 pages." The facilitator then asks volunteers to state what information they received. When parents who received the information that their child will be taught only 50 pages learn that other children will be taught more, they ask: "Why? What does it mean that my child is taught only 50 pages? Who made that decision?" This exercise is followed by another in which parents are told that their child received a grade of A. Parents then ask: "What does the 'A' mean? Does it mean the same for the 100-page and 50-page curriculums?" The staff of the Right Question Project know that parents asking hard questions does not always lead to change. But it is a critical first step.[5]

The Right Question Project focuses on helping parents to advocate successfully for their children wherever they go to school. More numerous are networks that work with groups of parents on a school-by-school basis. Henry Levin's Accelerated Schools is one of these networks. Robert Slavin's Success for All Schools and James Comer's School Development Project are others, as are many community-based organizations that are part of the National Coalition of Advocates for Students.

These networks differ in their specifics but they agree on the parents' role. Parents in the network schools know their children's achievement matters, and they believe their children can achieve. They visit their children's schools and they know about their children's schoolwork. They learn about homework policies, and work with their children to see that assignments are completed. They work with teachers rather than revert to mutual suspicion.

Most of these efforts are relatively new. The quality is sometimes uneven. But enough activities are underway to ensure that parents don't have to live in East Austin to get help in improving their children's education.

FROM HEALTH TO SKILLS

Getting the school-based health services was a milestone in the relationship between Zavala teachers and parents. As teachers saw parents taking the bus to come to the school board meeting, they began to view Zavala families in a different way. Hearing T. A. Vasquez and Anna Aquino speak articulately to a large group about the importance of health services at the school gave teachers a new sense of what such parents might accomplish. As Zavala parents watched the teachers come to the school board meeting and stay late into the night, they began to realize that the teachers cared about their children. For both groups, the victory was a powerful indication that by working together they could improve the lives of Zavala children.

It was time to address the issue of student achievement.

In January 1993 Austin Interfaith held a workshop for Zavala parents on the meaning of achievement test scores, with one session in English and another in Spanish. Fifty parents attended and came away with three messages:

- In the first grade, Zavala children scored about as well on the TAAS as other Austin children. These first-grade scores supported parents' belief that their children were capable of learning.
- Each year they were in the school, Zavala students fell further behind citywide averages. The parents began to

discuss why this should be so and came up with a range of explanations, from Zavala's curriculum and instruction to how children spent their time outside school.

- By the fourth grade, Zavala children scored so low on the TAAS that they were effectively eliminated from the competitive middle-school program and from Austin's high-quality high school magnet programs.

Learning these details was harder than learning about school-based health care. In the words of Lourdes Zamarron, "We did not realize the importance of the test score for our kids. . . . It was an eye-opener for us . . . we realized in this workshop that the report card might tell us one thing, and the test scores tell us another different story about our kids." For T. A. Vasquez, the workshop provided a similar message: "At that time, I thought things were fine. . . . If your kid's on the A-B honor roll, then everything must be hunky-dory, . . . but we weren't getting the full picture."

Joe Higgs, who led the workshop, argued that its timing was critical. Had the workshop been held before the health clinic victory, it would have set parents and teachers against each other. With the trust established by their success in winning the health services battle, parents and teachers could confront the children's low achievement without blaming each other. To the contrary, the two groups ended the workshop by agreeing that low achievement was a serious problem that they must solve together.

Backed by parents, Al Melton and the Zavala teachers took a number of steps to raise student achievement. They participated in training designed to change the organization of instruction and take better advantage of the small class sizes made possible by priority schools funding. The cooperative-learning training emphasized techniques for grouping together more able and less able children, for encouraging peer tutoring, for designing activities that encouraged children to learn from one another, and for making every child feel responsible for learning. Projects in which children learn from each other are typically not undertaken in schools. Yet, as the example of the Sharpshooters illustrates, the ability to work productively in groups is one of the New Basic Skills demanded by high-wage employers.

Zavala introduced a new language arts and mathematics curriculum that had a track record of improving achievement for disadvantaged children. In Austin, this curriculum had been restricted to children designated as gifted and talented, but Melton obtained a waiver, allowing Zavala to use it with all its children.

Melton and the teachers integrated all special-needs children into regular classrooms, freeing up resources that had been restricted to special-needs classes. The move contributed to a spirit that Zavala was committed to raising the achievement of all its children.

The teachers met to coordinate instruction across grade levels. The teachers in the upper grades explained the skills that they felt all the children needed, and the primary-grade teachers negotiated the grade levels at which each type of skills would be taught. At a firm like Honda, such conversations are routine: they are how production associates learn from each other to improve performance. In the typical U.S. school, such conversations are rare; teachers work in isolation and practice suffers accordingly.

Change continued. In September 1993 Zavala opened an afterschool program with more than 30 different course offerings, including a math club, an author's club, karate, sewing, and a very popular magic class. Three hundred of the 450 students at Zavala participated, and the program provided a variety of new roles at Zavala for parents.

The crown jewel of these efforts was the Zavala Young Scientists Program. The best of Austin's magnet programs is the LBJ High School Science Academy. For a Zavala child, getting to the Academy was a very long road. Zavala ended in the fifth grade. All students were then bussed to sixth grade at Murchison Middle School in affluent northwest Austin. Sixth graders who excelled there could transfer to the seventh- and eighth-grade science magnet program at Kealing Junior High School and finish at LBJ. Kealing Junior High is only one mile from Zavala—a short, easy trip. But Zavala students did poorly at Murchison, and in the last 10 years only one student had made it to Kealing.

Todd McDowell, the young science teacher, had an idea for improving the access of Zavala's students to the Kealing magnet program. He proposed that Zavala develop a sixth-grade science-intensive program that would prepare students for admission to the Kealing magnet program. As he said:

> Since my second year here, I was looking for something . . . to put Zavala on the map. . . . It occurred to me that what happens to our kids [after] fifth grade is that they go to northwest Austin, . . . probably the most affluent neighborhood in our city. Our kids are bussed over to that school for sixth grade, and the actual science program in the city is right over here around the corner at Kealing, but it starts at seventh grade. . . . There's this one-year gap where our kids go to the other side of the moon, and we lose them. . . . So it occurred to me that if we had a sixth-grade class here of the kids that were really interested in the stuff, and then got them . . . qualified to get into Kealing, it would make everybody's life a lot easier and it would be a lot more beneficial

to the children. So all the kids [in the Zavala sixth-grade science program] would go to Kealing, and the kids who didn't make it into the magnet classes would be put in honors classes, . . . and if they did well, then in eighth grade they could apply for the magnet.

Since the program could serve only some of the 50 students in Zavala's three fifth-grade classes, it was not obvious that Zavala parents would want it. Al Melton and the Zavala teachers asked Austin Interfaith to explore parents' reactions to the proposal. Joe Higgs and Kathleen Davis organized several meetings at which parents discussed the program and issues related to admission criteria if the program was developed. Out of these came strong support for a sixth-grade science program. As Rachel Gonzales described the meetings: "I can almost speak for most of the parents that . . . it was okay if our child was not selected . . . as long as Zavala gave the opportunity to one of our children's classmates."

Obtaining school board approval for this program was not easy. The board had a policy of promoting grade 6 to 8 middle schools and the Zavala proposal ran counter to it. Once again Zavala parents, with the support of Austin Interfaith, united to pressure the school board to support a community goal. Again the bus rides to the school board meeting and the carefully orchestrated speeches explaining why the program was critical to the Zavala community paid off, and one sixth grade, which became known as the Zavala Young Scientists Program, started in the fall of 1993.

Once established, the program attracted outside support: computers from Dell Computer and funds for extra resources from the National Science Foundation. The University of Texas provides supplies, a mentor for each participating student, and field trips to the University. In a high-income suburb, McDowell's program would be good but not unusual. In schools like Zavala, it is very rare: the kind of program parents don't think teachers will offer and teachers don't think parents care about. In 1994, six of the 17 children in the Zavala Young Scientists program were admitted to the Kealing magnet program. In 1995, seven were admitted.

LASTING CHANGE AT ZAVALA?

In the retrospective glow of success, change at Zavala doesn't seem so hard. Sixteen teachers left Zavala at the end of 1990–91. No one left at the end of the 1993–94 or 1994–95 school years. In 1990–91, Zavala ranked 33 in attendance among 63 Austin elementary schools. In 1993–94, it tied for first in attendance, and in 1994–95 it was undisputed champion with 97.8 percent attendance. In both these years, the percentage of Zavala students who passed the TAAS in reading and mathematics was higher than the citywide averages.

In the course of these changes, all of the Five Principles had been implemented. The story began with the First Principle: by parents and teachers and children agreeing that Zavala was bad and that Zavala could be good. This first principle was essential; agreement on goals was necessary for progress. But progress toward these goals required the other principles as well. The new governance structure gave parents and teachers opportunities to contribute to solutions. Teachers got the training they needed to change how children spent their time in classrooms. Attendance records, TAAS scores, and admissions to Kealing were measures of progress critical to demonstrating that the efforts of parents, teachers, and students were making a difference. Perseverance and learning from mistakes were necessary to sustain the change effort in the face of a variety of initial setbacks.

Ten years ago, Zavala belonged to the Austin school department. Today it belongs to the teachers and parents, too: T. A. Vasquez walks into the teachers' room, grabs a cup off the shelf, and pours herself coffee; Rachel Gonzalez hugs one of the school's janitors in a chance meeting in a Zavala hallway; Anna Aquino works with teachers on the school's health committee to be sure that all children are immunized; Lourdes Zamarron interviews candidates for a teaching position, knowing that only an applicant receiving the unanimous support of the hiring committee, including parents, will be hired.

With this support, teachers can ask more of the children. City government has to take the school more seriously. But the most important aspect of parental support is that it didn't exist five years ago. It had to be nurtured to the point where parents could visit Zavala for positive reasons, not just because their child was in trouble.

Will Zavala's improvements last? Al Melton typically arrives at Zavala at 6:30 A.M. and stays until 7:00 P.M. He works all day Saturday and often part of Sunday. How long can he sustain this pace? Most of the parents who were central to the changes at Zavala will turn their attention to other issues after their children move into higher grades. Is it reasonable to expect Zavala's progress will continue?

The question has no simple answer, but two initiatives give some hope of continuity. The first is Austin Interfaith itself. Joe Higgs and Kathleen Davis are working to build support for Austin Interfaith into the core activities of its member parishes. If successful, their work will provide continued financial support for full-time organizers to work with successive generations of Zavala families. It would also link Zavala with the constituencies of churches and with their political clout.

The second initiative is the Alliance Schools Network, the network begun in 1992 by Ernie Cortes, of which Zavala parents and teachers are an active part. Every year, parents and teachers from the Alliance meet to discuss successes and setbacks and to reaffirm their commitment to change. The Alliance meetings are rare events in this country: hundreds of low-income parents, most of them Afro-American or Hispanic, meeting with public school teachers and administrators to discuss how they can work together to improve their schools. The meetings along with local forums are attempting to build institutions that will outlast the individuals in each school.

Earlier, we described how people are slowly building parent organizations committed to skills for all children well beyond the state of Texas. This is good news, since roughly half of the nation's 17-year-olds now lack mastery of the New Basic Skills (Chapter 2). Since the economy's pressure will continue, most U.S. schools need to change. But change is unlikely in any school until the First Principle is applied: Get the frontline workers—beginning with the parents and the teachers—to agree on the problem.

CHAPTER 5

THE SECOND PRINCIPLE
PROVIDE THE RIGHT INCENTIVES
AND OPPORTUNITIES

THE RUSSIAN NAILS

When the Soviet economy was run by central planning, a story was told of a nail factory in Smirsk, a factory quite different from Diamond-Star or Honda. This nail factory, like other Soviet factories, received its production quota from Moscow: 10 metric tons of nails. And like other Soviet firms, the nail factory had strong incentives to meet its quota—which it did, by making 10 nails, each weighing one metric ton. This apocryphal story illustrates the importance not only of caring about incentives, but also of getting the incentives right.

The story would be funny if it didn't fit U.S. schools so well.

On a map, the distance from Boston High School to the laboratories of Massachusetts General Hospital (MGH) is not very great—a 1.5-mile walk that winds through the Boston Commons and Beacon Hill. In mental terms, the journey is longer. Boston High is a tough, career-preparation school, largely minority, where students take classes for half the day and work the other half. MGH is a leading teaching hospital, largely white and very white collar, with good jobs ranging from laboratory technicians to neurosurgeons—but only for people with skills.

For students to make this journey, lots of people have to take initiative. Teachers must understand the math, science, and communication skills required of a laboratory technician and bring those skills into the classroom. Students must make the extra effort to learn the new material. Hospital supervisors have to go out of their way to help students make what for many is a very big adjustment.

Firms like Diamond-Star, Honda, and NML rely on incentives that encourage frontline workers to take such initiative. But the incentives in the typical U.S. high school, like the incentives in the nail factory, are not so constructive. More often than not, they encourage students and teachers to turn inward, away from the economy. The journey from school to a good job never begins. Getting a school's incentives right—the Second Principle—is a journey in itself. The story of the Boston ProTech program illuminates what is involved.

It is the spring of 1994, and Domingus Barbosa—Tony to those who know him—is preparing bone sections for use in laboratory slides. Tony, a part-time lab technician, is a slender 19-year-old with a sly, humorous face. He lives with his father and stepmother, immigrants from the Cape Verdean Islands. Tony is a Boston High School graduate, class of 1993, and a member of the first class of Project ProTech, a youth apprenticeship program that began operation in the spring of 1991.

It is a good time for Tony. He has just finished his first year at Mt. Ida Junior College in suburban Newton. He is the first member of his family to go to college, and the year went reasonably well. A year ago, he had planned to enroll at Mt. Ida to become a physical therapist. By the end of the first semester, he had switched to criminal justice and a more academic curriculum, including courses in science and psychology. The skills Tony acquired in high school left him fairly well prepared: "[The courses] weren't easy but they weren't so hard that I couldn't do them." His average for the year was C+. And there was the lab job:

> The hours are flexible, you know. You don't have any set time you have to come in. . . . Say I come in today, the guy tells me we need some sections on this type of bone—say 17-day-old rats. I go to the freezer and I'll get the rats and cut off the leg—you use the hind leg and the tibia bone. I'll cut it and bring it to my old lab. They embed it and I bring it up here and I cut it with a microtoner and make the slides. . . . You come in, you put in your hours for the day, you leave. I like that.

The job in the Endocrine-Molecular-Histology Lab is Tony's second or third job at MGH, depending on who is counting. His first position, an unpaid internship, was in radiology. It had come in the spring of 1992, when Tony was a junior at Boston High and a first-year ProTech apprentice. Tony chose the radiology job after five months of hospital orientation. It could have become a long-term assignment—the kind Tony has now. But there were frictions between Tony and his supervisor. "One week I would do this and then they would send me somewhere else, and I didn't get the hands-on experience I wanted. . . . They would just have me stand there and listen."

Tony was not alone in feeling that the ProTech jobs had problems. Lois Ann Porter, the ProTech director on the staff of the Boston Private Industry Council, explains: "We set off on a course that first year, purely by the seat of our pants. You know—we were creating, and ideas were flowing, [but] the kids were actually already in place. So for the students' sake, for the schools' sake, for the employers' sake, it was really a tough year."

At the end of his junior year, Tony transferred into the Histology/Pathology Laboratory directed by Mike Frederickson. Mike is about 40, smart and fair, with a strong sense of how his lab should be run. Tony blossomed under Mike, learning how to use the lab's tools and to accurately make and record tests. Mike gives Tony all the credit: "In his first year, anything we asked him to do, he did. Even the scut work. He always did what we asked, but he was always asking how to do other jobs, too. By the second year, he could do as much as most of my regular employees. He and Darryl [another ProTech apprentice] really give a lift to the other people in the lab."

Tony changed hospital jobs again in January 1994 at the end of his first semester at Mt. Ida. Earlier in that month, Tony had gotten a call from Michelle Fredette, a senior recruiter at MGH and the hospital's ProTech point person. As Tony recalls:

> Michelle said, "We heard you changed your major to criminal justice. There's nothing wrong with that, you know, but it's not in the ProTech program. So you have to leave the job [in Mike's lab]." Which I can understand.
>
> But out of coincidence, she told me about this job. She said, "There's this lab job that's open, and you'd be doing the same things you're doing now." And the job is at Massachusetts General [a job on the regular payroll], so you're paid at Mass. General wages—not ProTech wages." So I

came in and filled in an application, and Mike wrote me a recommendation.

Tony expects to receive an Associates' Degree in Criminal Justice. He then plans to transfer to a four-year college to complete his education.

A COLLECTION OF BAD INCENTIVES

Tony is a walking success story, a teenager from a low-income family on his way to a middle-class career. But Tony had advantages. As a freshman he was selected for extra math and science courses at nearby Franklin Institute. At the end of his sophomore year, Tony applied and was chosen for the first class of Boston ProTech. Through these various programs, Tony acquired some of the New Basic Skills: math skills, reading skills, an ability to reason through a problem, an ability to communicate (Chapter 2). Tony also received firsthand knowledge about good jobs. This makes Tony unusual. Many teenagers graduate from high school without acquiring these things.

Some of this failure is no mystery. Begin with the lack of good job knowledge. Today, one child in four comes from a family with an income below $20,000. Few of these families have parents with middle-class jobs. Some have no working parent at all. For some of these children, learning about good jobs in the old-fashioned way—from dinner table conversation—is not easy.

The failure of schools to teach about good jobs is more mysterious—until we examine the incentives teachers face. Pam McDonnell is a Boston High School science teacher who is clearly interested in her students. Pam's job description includes teaching, taking attendance, and grading tests. It doesn't include determining the science skills required of a health technician. If Pam wanted to discover those skills, she would have to locate the right hospital supervisors and have the conversations on her own time.

Most high school teachers face similar incentives with a predictable result: they learn about the job market for high school teachers and few other middle-class jobs. The teachers are not evil or lazy. They respond to the incentives they face. What makes Pam McDonnell's case different is that ProTech began to change those incentives.

Bad incentives also help explain why many students graduate without adequate skills. The United States is a country of second chances where people can experiment until they find their niche. When applied to schools, the logic of the second chance led to two organizational goals:

> Keep students from dropping out; the lack of a diploma forecloses options. Avoid occupational learning that might force students into early, irrevocable choices.

For many students, maintaining options means going to school in the general curriculum track, a watered-down college-preparation track in which standards are kept low to keep students in school. Classrooms settle into unspoken treaties in which teachers do not assign hard material or heavy homework in exchange for students coming to class and not making trouble.[1] Serious mathematics, serious writing, working in groups to define problems and develop solutions—these and the rest of the New Basic Skills—are too much to ask.

Classroom treaties may not include high grades. When

ProTech began to select the first apprentices in the spring of 1991, participating hospitals had hoped for students who had at least B's in math, science, and English, an overall C+ average, and 90 percent attendance. They found that in the ProTech schools—three of the city's weaker high schools— only 12 percent of the students could meet those standards.[2]

But with or without good grades, classroom treaties lead to the worst of both worlds: a high school education that is short on both skills and knowledge about good jobs. The student's only gain is not having to work very hard. How does such a perverse system continue? Through the late 1970s, when most high school graduates got good jobs (Figure 2.1), treaties were the path of least resistance. But how can treaties persist today, when so many high school students earn so little? Here, too, the answers lie in the incentives facing students and teachers.

Start with students. The incentives facing students are shaped in part by employers, few of whom pay much attention to what applicants did in school. B. J. Holtzapple is the registrar of the well-regarded Bethesda–Chevy Chase High School in suburban Washington, D.C. Although many of its graduates go on to college, a significant fraction go directly to work. In 1992, we asked Holtzapple how many times she had been called by employers during the previous year to request an applicant's transcript. She smiled. "Why don't you ask me how many times they called just to see if a kid graduated?" "Okay," we said: "How many times?" Holtzapple replied: "Only once or twice. For kids who take jobs that need security clearance. Nobody else calls about graduation or transcripts."

Recall from Chapter 2 that students' knowledge of mathematics plays a growing role in wages at age 24, but not at age 20. B. J. Holtzapple's observation helps to explain why. High-wage employers assume that most teenagers are immature. Like Diamond-Star, Honda, and NML, these firms know that exceptions exist, but they view it as expensive, and perhaps legally risky[3] to screen for the exceptions. If they hire any recent high school graduates, they hire them for low-level jobs on the basis of superficial characteristics: presentability, apparent reliability. Transcripts are not considered. The employers then observe the young people over time to identify candidates for promotion to serious jobs— Mary Grace James and Karen Pawlak at Northwestern Mutual Life.[4] So skills count, but only in the long term. Students, many of whom live in the short term, can't see the payoff to studying hard.

It doesn't have to be this way. In Japan many corporations have long-term relationships with selected high schools. The corporations rely on teacher recommendations in hiring two or three outstanding students each year into serious training programs. In this way, Japanese employers offer a strong incentive for students to acquire mathematics, literacy, and science skills which many U.S. students lack.

To this point, we have discussed the weak incentives facing students who go directly to work. What about students planning to go to college? Don't they have stronger incentives for serious learning? In some cases, yes. In many cases, no. Good grades, honors courses, and high SATs are needed for the upper tier of U.S. colleges—the colleges for which the best students in the college prep track compete. But if a student simply wants to go to college—any college—a mediocre record is not an obstacle. Polls of college freshmen by the UCLA Graduate School of Education show that across the nation, 75 to 80 percent of freshman say they are attending their first- or second-choice school.⁵ The high percentage contains some ex post rationalization but it shows that college attendance per se does not require high-intensity academic work. In this economy, these students, too, will eventually need math, reading, problem-solving, and communication skills—the New Basic Skills. But since many colleges do not demand these skills for admission, the incentive to learn them may be weak.

The incentives for teachers to emphasize skills are not much stronger. Few high schools offer warranties on their graduates. If lack of skills causes a school's graduates to do poorly in the new job market, few teachers will hear about it, much less be penalized because of it. The structure of a teacher's job, with little time to explore employer requirements, reinforces the problem. From a school's perspective, student careers occur in the future but the dropout rate is here and now—an immediately measurable goal. Given this asymmetry, it is easy to see why schools work to keep the dropout rate down, whatever the cost in skills.

Recently several states have addressed incentives by rewarding teachers in schools with unexpectedly high student achievement and sanctioning teachers in schools with unexpectedly low achievement.⁶ These initiatives acknowledge the importance of incentives for teachers—a good first step. But by saying nothing about incentives for students, they contain a serious weakness. Teachers alone cannot improve student achievement if students see little reason to learn.

Compared to a firm like Diamond-Star Motors, the average U.S. high school is a collection of bad incentives. A person who would improve those incentives has a very full plate: creating incentives for teachers to learn about rising skill requirements, creating incentives for high-wage employers to learn about schools, creating incentives for students to do the harder work that mastery of the New Basic Skills requires. All of this raises another incentive question: Why should anyone want to take on this job?

THE ROOTS OF PROTECH

In Zavala Elementary School, the spur to action came from Austin Interfaith. In the case of Boston ProTech, the spur came from Boston's business establishment through the Boston Private Industry Council (PIC). As befits established institutions, the business community's decision was not spontaneous.

The decision had roots in the 1960s, when Boston began a massive effort to renew itself and to attract new business. The Boston public schools were an obvious roadblock. The system maintained certain jewels—the entrance-by-examination Boston Latin School—but its overall reputation was weak. By the end of the 1960s, weakness had turned into something worse with the battles over court-ordered bussing. Students were moving to parochial schools and the suburbs at accelerating rates.

The business establishment responded to this decline by creating business-school partnerships. Theresa Feeney teaches computers and business to ProTech financial students at Charlestown High School. She was at Charlestown High in the 1970s as well: "We had a [precursor of] ProTech with Liberty Mutual Insurance Company. When bussing first began, they hooked all the high schools up with a business. And for many years, Liberty Mutual Insurance Company has been our business. They support us in many, many ways: financially and giving students jobs, it's just been a wonderful relationship over, I'd say, 15 years."

By 1983 the one-to-one pairings had evolved into the Boston Compact, an agreement brokered by the Private Industry Council between the public schools and business. Under the compact, business would provide summer jobs for eligible students, entry-level jobs for graduates, and the money for career counseling positions. The schools would raise student achievement levels, improve teaching, and lower the dropout rate. It was, however, an arms-length relationship: teachers did not visit the workplace, nor did business become involved in curriculum.

Today the Boston Compact places 3,300 students in summer jobs, 900 students in afterschool jobs, and participating firms hire significant numbers of the system's graduates. Nevertheless, by the late 1980s the business community found the arrangement wanting. Neither student achievement scores nor the dropout rate had improved very much. The Massachusetts economy was booming and the Compact's incentive for students—entry-level jobs—was not very powerful. Beyond this, business leaders were beginning to see that a standard high school diploma was no longer enough. Because of the boom, the wages of Massachusetts high school graduates were higher than those of graduates elsewhere. But people knew that the boom would end and Massachusetts would soon resemble the rest of the country. There had to be a different kind of program to prepare students for the rising skill requirements of middle-class jobs. But until there was broader agreement on the problem (the First Principle), nothing could be accomplished.

Helped by the PIC, a small group of Boston business leaders and Boston school administrators held a series of meetings and embarked on a trip to Europe to look at various apprenticeship programs. Participants were particularly attracted to the German apprenticeship model, which, as analyst Sue Goldberger writes, "offered an ideal vehicle to transform a job placement partnership into a comprehensive training system."[7]

German apprenticeships could not be copied whole cloth; they depended too much on German institutions, including a strong union movement. Instead, ideas began to converge on an "Americanized apprenticeship" with four components:

- A part-time job (usually full-time in the summer) on a career ladder—an apprentice technician like Tony Barbosa or a nursing assistant like Tony's classmate Trecia White. The crucial element is that the part-time job clearly leads somewhere desirable.

- A structured relationship between the student's employer and school. Both the school and the employer would have a voice in who gets and who keeps the apprenticeship jobs, the procedure for breaking students into the job, whether there is academic instruction at the jobsite, and so on.

- A revised in-school curriculum that allowed students to learn material that was relevant to their jobs. The curriculum might include job-specific skills, but most important, it would use work-related examples to motivate interest in broad-based academic skills such as mathematics and writing.

- Strong encouragement for the student to attend a junior college or four-year college. If the student attended a local college and continued to major in the apprenticeship field, he or she would, like Tony, have access to continued counseling and be allowed to continue in the job.

APPRENTICESHIPS, ACADEMIES, AND TECH PREPS

Boston was not the only place arriving at these principles. In various combinations, the principles underlie a small but growing number of school-to-work programs with a variety of names: youth apprenticeships like ProTech, Tulsa's Craftsmanship 2000, and the Pennsylvania Youth Apprenticeship program; career academies in Baltimore, New York City, Los Angeles, Pasadena, Philadelphia, and Oakland; tech prep programs in Rhode Island and South Carolina; restructured vocational education programs in Cambridge, Massachusetts, and Fort Collins, Colorado. Among them, the programs emphasize careers in health care, financial services, aerospace, electronics, precision metalworking, printing, and tourism. Many youth apprenticeships (like ProTech) put their first efforts into developing jobs; classroom change comes later. Many career academies put their first efforts into curriculum change and develop workplace experience in summer jobs.[8] Some programs are housed in their own buildings. Others are run as schools-within-schools where the program's students take all their classes together. In still others, students take the school's standard program with only a few separate classes.

Despite their differences, these programs have a common goal: to restructure a school's incentives so that students learn the skills required for good jobs. This is different from traditional vocational education. Traditional programs teach students the details of a specific job. The new programs use specific jobs to motivate a hidden agenda of mathematics, communication, and problem solving—the New Basic Skills valued throughout the economy.

Getting a program off the ground is no easy job. Begin with teachers. If a teacher is to motivate student interest in mathematics through workplace examples, the program must get teachers into the workplace. These visits are not easy to arrange. They often take place in the summer to avoid conflicts with rigid school schedules and union work rules. But the visits do occur.

The program must get employers to learn more about adolescents and begin to see the world through a teacher's eyes: how, for example, to talk to a previously reliable apprentice who wanted to skip work unannounced because her family was evicted from their home and she spent last night on the street.

If the program takes root, the incentives facing students will improve. The fact that the school controls admission to the program further strengthens the incentive to learn. When teachers motivate academic subjects with workplace examples, students can better understand the point of learning algebra or preparing an oral report. Realistic problems at work or in class can provide opportunities for active learning, the "hands-on, minds-on" process in which students can learn abstract ideas by doing things rather than sitting and taking notes.

Finally, a successful program can create student knowledge about good jobs. In career academies, the knowledge comes through summer jobs and discussions with recruiting officers. In apprenticeships like ProTech, the knowledge comes from the apprentice jobs. Tony and his classmates—Dawn Moore, Trecia White, and LaToya Joyce, who worked as nursing assistants; Scott Reynolds, who worked as a radiology assistant; Billy deJesus, who worked as a nuclear medicine assistant; and others—were face-to-face with well-paying white-collar jobs they could attain if they learned the New Basic Skills. Some of the apprentices were auditioning: letting an employer know who they were far better than any transcript would reveal. Others, like Tony, would not continue in health care. But most of the apprentices would learn about the connections among work and skills and wages, something many students never learn.

In all of these ways, the new school-to-work programs can significantly improve a school's incentives *if* the program gets up and running and *if* the program runs as promised. To reach that point, someone needs to do a big selling job to employers, schools, and students. And then someone needs the perseverance to fix the bugs that any new program will have.

SELLING THE HOSPITALS

In Boston, the PIC was doing the selling and the first buyers came from the city's 16 teaching hospitals. While business leaders and educators were touring German apprenticeships, Boston hospitals were scrambling for technicians and nurses, both in short supply. Hospital administrators were forced to raise salaries even as they were trying to contain costs. In this squeeze, they were interested in any program that might produce more skilled workers.

It was a short step from interest to action. Hospital chief executive officers filled three of the 16 seats on the PIC board, including the chairmanship. The chairman, Dr. Jerome Grossman, head of the New England Medical Center, worked hard to recruit other hospitals to the cause. The

experience of the Boston Compact helped. As Lois Ann
Porter said:

> Four out of the first six hospitals in ProTech had been long-
> term employers of youth providing afterschool and summer
> jobs for students. So that wasn't foreign to them either. . . .
> What they weren't getting, though, was any sort of return
> on that in any employability way. . . . They were getting . . .
> the feel-good stuff. What they weren't getting were higher-
> qualified applicants from the Boston Public Schools for the
> jobs within the health care industry . . . only 1 percent of
> graduates of the Boston public schools were going into
> allied health, even though health had 17 or 18 percent of
> workers in the city.

One hospital administrator made the same point: "We
are involved in so many do-good things. This is one do-good
thing that will also work for us. . . . We've been involved in
so many school-partnership and youth-employment projects
that haven't been effective. If you're going to do a partnership, you might as well do it right. ProTech is a chance to do
something comprehensive and meaningful."[9]

In one way, ProTech's startup was typical. Among 16
school-to-work programs examined by the Manpower
Development Research Corporation, organizations like the
PIC took an early lead in seven. The Tulsa Chamber of
Commerce worked to recruit employers to the Tulsa Youth
Apprenticeship program; the Portland Chamber of Com-
merce created the Business Youth Exchange to work with
the Portland schools' Occupational Cluster program; the
Oakland, California, Alliance worked with Oakland Techni-
cal High School to establish the school's health academy.[10]

What was different about ProTech was the initial lack of
school involvement. Among those same 16 programs, school

administrators and/or teachers were early leaders in 12. In some sites, the school people began alone. In other sites, schools quickly joined with organizations like the PIC. But in Boston, ProTech first took shape without the schools. Since ProTech was ultimately about education, the lack of school involvement was not a good sign.

SELLING THE SCHOOLS

ProTech should have been good for schools because it rips up classroom treaties. When a student volunteers for a school-to-work program, teachers can reasonably demand more work. If the program runs well, the student will have stronger incentives to do that work, making the teacher's job that much easier.

Less obviously, programs like ProTech create a socially acceptable way for students to learn serious skills—the hidden agenda again. Enrollees can cluster together in classes where most people are interested in learning. Because the classes are job-related, a student can study chemistry or pre-calculus without being ostracized for "acting snobbish" or, in the case of minority students, "acting white." Upon visiting the Philadelphia Health Academy at Overbrook High School, one astute observer, a union specialist, remarked: "This isn't a real [union-like] apprenticeship. This is a good college-prep program with a health care overlay." Natalie Allen, director of Philadelphia High School Academies Inc., implicitly agreed: "I don't want us to be judged by the number of students who go on to health care professions per se. If students go on to higher education in other professions, if students have good academic outcomes, that is okay with us even if they're not in health."

A cynic might dismiss such a program as serving motivated students who would do well in any case. But the typical ProTech student is neither a "success" nor a "failure." Rather, they are teenagers on the cusp: being in classes where most students want to learn can make all the difference.

But a program can only achieve these benefits if it reaches a critical mass—enough participating students in a school to take most of their classes together. "Block scheduling" in school jargon is not as simple as it sounds. The Boston public schools' tight budget dictates that most classes have 30 students. But as any administrator can tell you, trying to block-schedule with just 30 students won't work, since some students are scheduled to take Algebra II while others are scheduled for Geometry and so on.

Without critical mass, a school can block-schedule apprentices for only one or two classes. Most other classes will have 10 or 12 apprentices mixed in with 18 regular students. Under these conditions teachers have little incentive to develop a new curriculum or to change teaching methods. For many of the teachers, the program is just "one more thing" the schools are being asked to do, and not much of a lever for change.

ProTech began in Boston High and two other schools, none with a critical mass. The reasons were not all bad. Despite the hospitals' interest, ProTech began with a total of just 75 apprentice slots. Since ProTech's ultimate goal was to improve the city's high schools, it chose to spread these slots among several schools rather than to concentrate them in one place. But mixed in with this good reason was ProTech's failure to involve the schools in program design, a failure that left school people indifferent at best. Lois Ann Porter:

We started on the wrong foot with the schools, quite honestly. We were approached by the businesses, we worked initially with the businesses, the businesses were part of the design. And we issued [an invitation for schools to participate] in which we said: "We have created this structure. If you want to create a situation that meets our criteria, we will select you." That set up a dynamic. . . . [The schools] hadn't been any part of the process up to that point. There was a lot of healing that had to take place . . . not only because of the dynamic but because of the skepticism that ProTech was just another new program.

Theresa Feeney of Charlestown High, the ProTech financial services teacher, echoed this skepticism:

You know, we face a lot here. This whole thing is like reinventing the wheel. I mean, there were business programs in place [in the 1970s], and kids were really trained well in business. The school didn't get them a job, they got their own jobs. But that is basically what it was—it was training kids who weren't going to go on to college. And then all that stopped. Money got cut and programs got cut, so the first thing they cut in Boston was business teachers. All gone . . .

When it was all happening, they said, "The businesses are going to train the kids themselves." And it hasn't worked out. The businesses don't train the kids. They don't have time to train them.

No school-to-work program has had an easy start, but few have faced all ProTech's obstacles. The first Philadelphia Career Academy was an electronics program in Thomas Edison High School. As a school-within-a-school, it focused on classroom instruction. Because the academy did not use apprenticeships, its growth was not limited by the availability of supervised apprenticeships. And because the school system was a partner from the start, the academy began with a solid institutional foundation. Over time, getting Pro-Tech on a strong foundation would become an increasingly high priority.

SELLING THE STUDENTS

To a middle-class adult, ProTech health care apprenticeships looked like prepaid tickets to the middle class. To Boston High School sophomores in the spring of 1991, ProTech looked more problematic.

ProTech was built around paid jobs—15 hours per week at $5.50 per hour beginning late in the student's junior year. But Boston High School is a career high school where students are expected to work in the afternoons, and the school helps them to find work. A student who just wanted a job had other options, some of which paid more.

Then there was the content. Some students knew that health care was not for them. Others worried about having to take harder courses, including, in ProTech's start-up year, courses at a neighboring community college. The fact that ProTech was new with no reputation or graduates further increased its risk.

The job of selling ProTech to Boston High students fell to a ProTech counselor, paid by the PIC and assigned full-time to the school. The first resigned after a year. In September 1992, at the start of ProTech's second full year, Phillisa Prescott, a warm, energetic woman who had previously worked with youth in a psychiatric hospital, and later in a halfway house for juvenile offenders who were nearing release, became Boston High's ProTech Counselor. Phillisa knew about tough kids.

In the spring of 1993, Phillisa recruited ProTech's third class through various routes. With Michelle Fredette, the MGH administrator, she held a recruiting assembly for sophomores. She had one-on-one conversations with sophomore class homeroom teachers to ask for potential applicants. She read through the folder of every Boston High sophomore and picked out likely candidates.

In fact, "likely candidate" was an imprecise term, since ProTech was too new to have a profile of a successful applicant. In the previous year, the hospitals' initial profile—90 percent attendance, B's in science and math, at least a C+ overall average—had been too selective to fill all available slots. In the end, the selectors had focused on strong attendance, a B in biology, and passing a personal interview. Through this process, 25 Boston High students had been selected.

Almost all school-to-work programs use similar recruiting programs:

- Market the program to all students in a school—not just the poor and disadvantaged.
- Rely on student self-selection as the first important screen.
- In choosing your applicants, remember what you are: a program that tries to teach better math, writing, and problem-solving skills—not just occupational specifics.[11]

The last point is part of the hidden agenda. Whatever these programs are, they are not remedial training. A program like Restructured Vocational Education in Cambridge,

Massachusetts, sees itself as important for the clearly college bound as for anyone else. The fraction of low-income students in a program will depend on the schools from which it draws. But in Boston High as elsewhere, the most disadvantaged students—for example, students with very weak attendance records—almost never get through the door.

The need for all this selling highlights the likelihood that a school's incentives cannot be changed one at a time. A youth apprenticeship program requires simultaneous investments from employers creating jobs slots in which learning takes place, from schools changing their scheduling and curriculum, and from students doing more work in harder courses. For the program to work, all the parties have to buy in, at least halfway. But none of the parties will want to buy in unless they know the others will buy in as well. This is part of the problem of Getting from Here to There, a problem discussed in Chapter 9.

FIRST-YEAR GLITCHES

When ProTech was being planned, it could be all things to all people—a magic bullet. Reality arrives when the program begins. Student, teacher, and employer expectations confront a brand-new program with glitches. Now is when the perseverance and learning start.

ProTech's glitches began in September 1991, when Tony Barbosa and his classmates, then juniors, began hospital orientation. Four months earlier, Tony had signed up for ProTech thinking he wanted to work in the health professions. But where in the health professions? None of the students had this kind of knowledge, yet getting a good fit between student and job was critical to program success.

The PIC and the hospitals had planned to solve this problem with a set of rotations in which the students would be exposed to five or six different job areas. The rotations would begin in September of the student's junior year, last through February, and mix work with observation and teaching. A completed rotation, good behavior, and a C+ average in the fall semester would allow the student to move into a hospital job.

For Tony, Trecia, and the rest of the Boston High apprentices, the rotations were ProTech's worst part. No one had told hospital staff to alter their routines for the students' sake. And so in each area the rotations dragged on, one day a week for four weeks. Hospital staff would work and the students would sit and watch. Hospital staff would lecture, and the students would sit and listen. The much discussed hands-on learning rarely occurred and students were unimpressed: "We couldn't do anything." "We couldn't work. We couldn't touch anything." "It was so boring." "We had no say in anything. Everything was mandatory."

Rotations were also the time when students first encountered hospital rules. To an adult ear, many of the rules were mundane: show up on time, no unexcused absences, always carry your identification card. To many of the kids, the rules were a big change. As Phillisa Prescott explained a year later: "From the students' perspective, they can get away with so much more at the school site than on the job. They know how many times they can be tardy [in school]. They know how much work they need to do to get a passing grade. At work, they can't get away with that. They may know that they can be absent 15 days a semester at school. But if they did that at work, they'd be gone long before they missed 15 days." There were also dress codes—no nose

rings, no tank tops or very short skirts, and for most supervisors, no hightops.

At bottom, each of the rules involved two issues: one
about appropriate behavior, the other about following a
supervisor's order. For Boston High students—even the better
students—taking orders had special significance. Most had
grown up in tough neighborhoods. All were going to a tough
high school. The strategy for survival was summarized by
Billy deJesus: "You don't take nothing off of nobody." To an
MGH supervisor, nose rings were about scaring patients. To
a Boston High School junior, nose rings were about respect.

Constantly moving between students and employer, the
ProTech counselors worked to solve the problems. Phillisa
Prescott was particularly adept. In the case of nose rings and
hightops, the students agreed: "Phillisa told us, we just had
to stick it out." And there was the case of the student whose
family had been evicted from its apartment the night before:
"He didn't want to go to work. He said: 'How can I go to
work when we don't even have a place to stay?' But I told
him: 'If you go to work, at least you'll keep some money
coming into your family. At least you'll have that.'" Phillisa
talked to the supervisor, and the student went to work.

ProTech survived its first year with a mixed record. By
June the work experience was looking more promising.
Rotations were over, and kids were now doing the work
they had come for. Tony had moved from the unsatisfactory
internship in radiology to the job in Mike Frederickson's lab.
Scott Reynolds was an assistant radiology technician and
enjoying the work. LaToya Joyce and Trecia White were
learning the routines of floor nurses. As Lois Ann Porter put
it: "Even though it was crazy, good things were happening."

ProTech's weakness was in fostering classroom change;

there was some, but not enough. Students took some courses they would otherwise not have taken—a year-long health sequence at Bunker Hill Community College. But Boston High's own courses changed very little. The program's small scale of operation was part of the reason; there were too few students for block scheduling. But the students had one block-scheduled course: Pam McDonnell's biology/physiology class. The course's unchanged content, despite Pam's interest, reflected another first-year glitch—getting teachers to the workplace.

In designing ProTech, the PIC and the hospitals had known that teachers needed to develop a new curriculum based on the workplace. Their proposed solution was work-site audits. In an audit, a teacher would be paid to visit a hospital for several days to observe various jobs that apprentices would hold. The teacher was then supposed to go home and use the observations to write new curriculum units.

Pam McDonnell went on one of these audits in July 1991, two months before the first ProTech apprentices began hospital orientation. The visit went well, but neither Pam nor the teachers from other schools had the experience or time to turn the observations into curriculum material. By the end of 1992, Pat Shelburne, a chemistry teacher at another ProTech school, had created a set of short worksite exercises. But little of this change made its way to Boston High.

Finally, the first year at Boston High suffered from program dropouts. Twelve of the original 25 juniors chose not to stay in ProTech as seniors. Several decided they did not like health work and moved to different jobs. Others argued the program was too much work. One became pregnant. Another said the program put her under too much pressure. Some of the attrition was predictable: most U.S. teenagers are discovering what they want to do. But some of the attrition reflected 10 years of bad schooling. Boston High's ProTech students were not the weakest in the school, but the move to MGH was still a bigger leap than some could handle.

Like all good managers, the people running ProTech knew few things worked well the first time. Even as ProTech was finishing its first year, PIC staff and the schools were planning improvements. In the second summer, more teachers were taken on worksite audits, but this time they were debriefed by curriculum writers who developed classroom materials. The fall-term rotations for juniors were shortened. The in-hospital lectures were abandoned. The in-school counselors were told to experiment with different recruiting methods. It was, in the language of good firms, continuous improvement.

The program's second year went better. Job rotations went more smoothly. Across the city, a few high school classes were starting to use serious workplace examples. On a sunny May morning in 1993, Brighton High School seniors were exploring the case of the emergency room admission of a policeman who had been in a fight with someone who might or might not have had AIDS, one of several problems they would work through that week.

But two years in the life of a school system is not very long, and ProTech, at bottom, was still an add-on—something the schools were willing to accept but not a school program per se. As outside employees, ProTech counselors operated with very little leverage. Everyone knew their grant funding might soon expire and they would be gone.

Both principals and the teachers' union refused to permit ProTech teachers to meet to coordinate teaching. In a firm like Diamond-Star, frontline workers are expected to solve problems together; that is how they learn from each other. In the Boston schools, principals refused to adjust in-school schedules for teacher meetings because it was inconvenient. The teachers' union refused to sanction afterschool meetings because they would be unpaid work. The message was that ProTech, whatever its goals, was too new and fragile to have much clout.

MOVING TO SOLID GROUND

The Cocoa Academy for Aerospace Technology in Cocoa, Florida, has 225 students in grades 10 to 12. Students spend much of their time in groups of five gathered around L-shaped desks. Each desk contains a networked personal computer with 16 megabytes of RAM. The curriculum is organized as a set of virtual learning activities (VLAs)— open-ended, complex tasks based on an engineering model of problem solving which includes a hands-on design, build, and test process. The VLAs were written by the academy faculty. Rather than lecture, the faculty work with individuals and groups of students as resources and coaches. Through the VLAs, students learn the mathematics, science, and writing skills embedded in the Florida curriculum frameworks as they devise solutions to the problems. The students tackle the VLAs in groups, learning the problem-solving and communications skills that are important in middle-class jobs today. While the academy is structured around the classroom, each student also completes an unpaid, mentored internship with a local aerospace firm.

In their gestations, Cocoa Academy and Boston ProTech are opposites. Cocoa Academy began in the classroom and slowly worked out; Boston ProTech began in the hospitals and is slowly working in. But the programs share a long-run problem: putting themselves on a solid foundation.

For Cocoa Academy, the central piece of a solid foundation is money. The Cocoa Academy is a part of Cocoa High School and so receives the average expenditure per student at the school. But the academy's start-up costs—summer pay for teachers to write curriculum and hardware purchases—were high. The program's ongoing cost per student is somewhat higher than in other Brevard County high schools. The director of the academy, Alexandra Penn, has been a successful fundraiser, and so far the academy has covered all its extra expenses with outside grants. But the academy's long-run stability depends on its getting into someone's budget—Brevard County's, the state of Florida's, or perhaps an industry trade group's. Without secure financing, at some point the program may fail.

For Boston ProTech, a strong foundation involves money and a number of other factors, beginning with the issue of job slots. Career academies like Cocoa Beach begin in the classroom. Youth apprenticeships like ProTech begin at work. But this ties ProTech to an economy where downsizing is a norm. In the early 1990s, Boston hospitals played a key role in getting ProTech started. Since then ProTech has added three more hospitals, but two of the largest hospitals have merged. No one believes such mergers have finished.

Through 1995, ProTech hospitals retained their commitments. But the PIC understood the necessity for diversification. In 1993 ProTech began a second set of apprenticeships in the city's financial services industry. In 1994, it began a third set of apprenticeships in utilities and communications. In the fall of 1995 apprenticeships began in environmental services. As was the case with hospitals, getting the job slots is just the beginning. The effort then shifts to ensure job quality—to ensure that jobs give students a reason to learn rather than use them as messengers or clerks. But ProTech's diversification is an important part of building long-term support.

ProTech faces two other long-term issues: building the curriculum and tightening connections with Boston Public Schools. The Cocoa Academy began as a project of the Brevard County public schools. Because its teachers were on the public school payroll, they could focus on academy business. ProTech's position was much more fragile—a nonschool project with modest leverage trying to change curriculum and teaching methods in existing high schools where teachers had multiple responsibilities. But ProTech persisted.

Beginning in 1994, the PIC replaced the summer worksite audits with larger Work and Learning programs. In Work and Learning, students and teachers spend a month together working half-days at a job site. The program was designed both to increase student learning and to develop curriculum materials. Unlike the earlier worksite audits, Work and Learning was financed by the state and the teacher salaries were funded by the Boston Public Schools, a sign that ProTech's stock was rising.

In another positive sign, the Boston public schools agreed to pay the salaries of four "school-to-career" lead teachers, each in a school housing ProTech. These teachers have responsibility for expanding school-to-work programs within the system.

There is much left to do. The salaries of the PIC staff—Lois Ann Porter and the ProTech counselors—still come from the U.S. Department of Labor. The funds are scheduled to end in 1996. As long as funding continues, Boston Pro-Tech is slowly losing its status as a hothouse flower. But Pro-

Tech's long-term survival will depend on the support of the Massachusetts state government, the Boston public schools, and the Boston business community.

Even if ProTech were to fully succeed, it would not be a panacea. The program begins in the tenth grade and so leaves education in the lower grades untouched. Of the 25 Boston High School students selected for ProTech's first class, 12 survived to graduate in June 1993. All 12, including Tony Barbosa, entered a two- or four-year college with financial aid, but three left during their first year because the coursework—particularly in the four-year colleges—was more than they could handle.

But if ProTech is not perfect, it offers insights into the Second Principle—providing the right incentives. Begin with the central idea: When high schools are connected to the larger economy, individual incentives begin to change. In the case of ProTech, the connection came through a student's chance to work in a job with a career path into the middle class. For many of the ProTech students, no one in their families or neighborhoods had ever held such jobs. Once the jobs were made real, the students' perception of school began to change and learning began to be relevant.

As ProTech evolved, it also embraced the other principles. ProTech could not have begun without agreement on the problem (the First Principle) first by the business community and then by the participating schools and faculty. It could not have survived without perseverance (the Fifth Principle) particularly on the part of the PIC.

Training (the Third Principle) was important, not always in expected ways. ProTech gave teachers the incentive to visit the workplace, but the teachers could not translate their observations into curriculum without the assistance of curriculum writers. Students were given the incentive to walk up good career paths, but without Phillisa Prescott's counseling and mediation, most students would have dropped out. Giving people incentives without training is as empty as giving people training without the incentives to use what they have learned.

There was, finally, ProTech's dependence on an ability to measure progress (the Fourth Principle). The high first-year dropout rate at Boston High showed quickly that program changes were needed—changes that enabled the program to survive past its first rocky year. The evidence of ProTech students graduating and moving on to college helped sustain the program and make the case for expansion. Without this visible evidence of progress, ProTech would likely have suffered the fate of most educational innovations and died a quiet death.

And along with the hard measures of progress come the soft stories that show that high schools indeed can change. Lois Ann Porter: "It's when the teachers sit at graduation and say, 'I never thought that student would graduate much less get a four-year scholarship to Northeastern.'" And Tony Barbosa, sitting at his lab table: "I mean, without the program, where would I have gotten these skills?"

CHAPTER 6

THE THIRD PRINCIPLE
TRAIN THE FRONTLINE WORKERS

I n the right environment people learn things all the time. In December 1991 Diann Buckner, Bill Bourbeau, and the Honda Sharpshooters represented Honda in the annual quality circle competition of the Ohio Manufacturers Association. Their subject was the stopped blower nut. They illustrated their presentation with the tools they had used—the Pareto charts, the cause-and-effect diagrams, and histograms. They showed how these tools were instrumental in discovering the source of the stopped blower nut and in devising potential solutions. The Sharpshooters then described their statistical analyses of attempted remedies that led them to reject the first five. They showed how the masking-tape solution had eliminated the stopped-blower-nut problem.

The presentation was an impressive display of technique. But when Honda hired Diann Buckner and Bill Bourbeau, neither was expected to know about Pareto charts or histograms. Honda was looking for the New Basic Skills: the reading and basic mathematics needed to understand training manuals and operating standards, the ability to communicate clearly, both in writing and orally, the ability to work with other people from varied backgrounds, an interest in solving problems that are not cut-and-dried.

In Honda's experience, someone with the New Basic Skills was likely to be a good worker. But someone with the New Basic Skills was also likely to benefit from Honda's training courses—to be a person who could learn, for example, how to use cause-and-effect diagrams to help solve problems.

Honda's emphasis on training is not unique. In many high-wage firms, the process of continuous product improvement requires frontline workers to continually solve new problems. Solving new problems requires learning new skills. The firms are willing to train workers in these skills provided the training meets two conditions:

- The skill being taught must improve the frontline worker's ability to achieve the firm's goals.
- The training itself must affect what the worker does. It cannot consist of a two-hour lecture without follow-up. Rather, training must include time for workers to discuss among themselves how a new skill is to be applied. And training must include reinforcement from persons ready to help frontline workers when the new application hits snags.

If difficult new problems provide the stimulus for training, U.S. schools should be the first in line to invest in training. The new problem is how to provide all students with the many-faceted New Basic Skills required to earn a middle-class wage. Of course, this is not the first new challenge that the schools have faced; socialization of waves of immigrants, racial integration, inclusion of handicapped children, and drug education are just a few of the previous challenges. All were difficult, but none involved teaching all students in new ways.

The job is not as hopeless as it appears. Psychologists are providing more and more information about how students learn and how best to teach them. Consider one backwater of current education, elementary school science.

In theory, science should have a high priority in elementary schools. A weak science background denies a child access to many technical careers and is important for that reason alone. But science is also important because it can be a powerful vehicle for teaching problem-solving skills.

Psychologists have shown that children learn science most effectively through "hands-on, minds-on" methods. At its best, hands-on science means children working in groups to formulate hypotheses, to design and carry out experiments, to collect and analyze data, to make inferences, and to communicate results in a clear and interesting way—the same activities performed by the Honda Sharpshooters. When children discover the principles that explain the data they have collected, they tend to remember those principles. A teacher's good questions can then help them see how to apply the principles to other situations.[1]

This is the good news—that effective methods exist to teach science in the elementary grades. The bad news is that few teachers teach this way. Instead, science instruction tends to consist of the teacher's talking and the student's being told to memorize scientific facts and complete worksheets. Susan Seymour, a fifth-grade teacher in Cabot, Massachusetts, described the way she was told to teach as a student teacher in Conover, a neighboring, affluent community:

"I was teaching science lecture fashion to these little third-graders. We were talking about Jupiter, and I would give them all these statistics, and they would take them down. Then they wrote a report. That is the way that unit is taught in Conover."

Why do teachers use "chalk and talk" teaching instead of hands-on teaching? One reason is that few elementary school teachers know much science, so they stick to the textbook as the safest approach. Another reason is that few elementary school teachers have had the experience of learning science through a "hands-on, minds-on" approach, and it is hard to give students an experience they have not had themselves. In his description of a remarkable second-grade teacher who accomplishes a great deal under trying conditions, Tracy Kidder captures the attitudes of many elementary school teachers: "She left science for last. For several other subjects she used textbooks, but only as outlines. She taught science right out of the book; this was one of those texts that takes pains with the obvious and gives the complex short shrift. Chris didn't know much science and didn't usually enjoy teaching it. Sometimes she let creative writing encroach on science's time. About one day in ten she canceled science altogether and announced—to cheers, Felipe's the loudest—an informal art lesson. She often felt guilty about science."[2]

Both the importance of elementary school science and its current weak condition are well known. From 1989 through 1993, Presidents Bush and Clinton and the nation's governors voiced support for an educational reform strategy labeled "Goals 2000" that stated in part: "By the year 2000, U.S. students will be first in the world in science and mathematics achievement" and "mathematics and science education . . . will be strengthened throughout the system, especially in the early grades."[3]

Setting the goals was not very difficult, even among contentious politicians. But actually reaching those goals will be. The quality of science teaching depends on today's teachers, most of whom were hired well before improving the science achievement of all children became a national goal. For these teachers, improving elementary science instruction is a new problem. And new problems require training.

RELEARNING TO TEACH

Many educators abhor the term "training." They argue that it implies a narrow focus inappropriate to the challenge. Changing the name has proved easy: what used to be called in-service training is now called professional development or staff development. Changing the substance has proved much harder.

Historically most professional development has taken one of two forms. Both are costly. Neither is very effective. The first are the annual "in-service days": students have a holiday and teachers attend a workshop at which an outside consultant presents a topic like new goals for mathematics instruction or new methods to promote cooperative learning. The topics are relevant to teachers' work. The lectures themselves are what good firms avoid: self-contained events with no follow-up through teacher discussions or outside reinforcement. Without the follow-up, in-service days rarely change what teachers do in the classroom.

The other form of professional development consists of university- or college-based courses that teachers take for graduate credit. Teachers have strong incentives to take courses because the salary schedules in most public school districts provide pay increments ranging from $1,000 to $10,000 for a master's degree and additional compensation for each 30 hours of graduate credit (10 semester-long courses) above the master's level.

Extra pay for taking graduate courses involves substantial money, but in most cases it is money not well spent. University-based courses seldom deal with the day-to-day work teachers do. Teachers may acquire significant knowledge from the courses, but the knowledge rarely translates into classroom change. Beyond course relevance, there is the issue of course quality. To attract paying customers, colleges and universities have incentives to offer courses that are convenient for teachers, fit their schedules, and do not put too many demands on their schedules. The result is a second kind of training that good firms avoid: potentially weak instruction in subjects with no particular relation to the organization's goals.

Contrast the opportunities typically available to teachers to improve their teaching with the opportunities provided to the associates at Honda of America. When Diann Buckner and Bill Bourbeau discovered a problem that was affecting their work, they requested permission to form a quality circle with two other associates to tackle the problem. As is the case with 9 out of 10 such requests, theirs was approved, and the Sharpshooters were in business tackling the stopped-blower-nut problem. The group met on company time for almost a year, diagnosing and solving the problem. They expected and received the support of other associates, most notably those in the paint department, in trying out possible solutions. When they had questions, they had ready access to experts who could answer them. They were expected to be clear about the problem they were trying to solve and to develop a strategy for assessing whether their work did indeed solve the problem. But they were not penalized for failure to solve the problem on their first try—in fact, it took six tries. When they completed their work, they received small financial rewards and credit toward the larger rewards that come from sustained problem-solving activities. Few teachers have such good opportunities and incentives to learn from their colleagues, and few work in environments where the importance of ongoing group problem solving by frontline workers is so appreciated as a strategy for improving quality.

Comparing training in best-practice firms with professional development in the average school presents quite a dismal picture. To make the comparison fairer, let's look at professional development in a school district with substantial advantages.

TEACHING THE PHYSICS OF LIGHT IN CABOT ELEMENTARY SCHOOLS

Cabot, Massachusetts, is an affluent community: median family income is $90,000, more than twice the statewide average. Median adult educational attainment is 16 years of schooling, 4 years above the statewide average.

Cabot has a long tradition of high-quality public schools. Nearly all students graduate from high school (compared to 80 percent nationally), and more than 95 percent of those graduates go on to college (compared to 60 percent nationally).

Per-pupil expenditures in the Cabot public schools average $7,000. Salaries start at $25,000 for a teacher with a bachelor's degree and no prior experience and extend to $58,000 for teachers with at least 15 years of experience and a master's degree plus 60 hours of additional course work (20 semester-long courses). One-quarter of Cabot's teachers are at the top of the salary scale. The school district's strong reputation and good salaries allow it to be extremely selective in hiring new teachers; in recent years there have been more than 1,000 applicants for the five to ten elementary school positions that become available each spring.

Well-educated parents, well-paid teachers, students who expect to go to competitive colleges, money for new initiatives—albeit less than in the past—make Cabot an extremely atypical American school district. If changing how teachers teach should be easy anywhere, it should be easy in Cabot.

As in most districts, especially affluent ones, the teachers in Cabot tend to be middle-aged; the average age is 47. Although there will be much more hiring over the next decade than there has been over the last, most teachers who will be at Cabot in the year 2000 are already there. When a school district plans to change what children learn, it must work with the teachers it already has.

Until recently, professional development at Cabot conformed to the traditional patterns described earlier. But the district also had a curriculum center staffed by specialists in particular subject areas, including science, mathematics, social studies, and language arts. In addition to providing advice on curriculum and teaching methods to elementary school teachers, the science specialist often taught the particularly challenging parts of the science curriculum. Although this arrangement ensured that many students received competent science instruction, it also meant that many classroom teachers never learned to teach science.

The limitations of the curriculum center approach became evident in the early 1980s, when budget cuts led to the dismissal of the science specialist and left elementary school teachers to their own resources in teaching science. For a few teachers this meant no change, since they had always taught the science curriculum themselves. For most, however, dismissal of the specialist forced them to teach material that they did not understand well or know how to teach. Some simply substituted other curricula for the science that had been taught by the specialists. As long as science was not seen as a critical part of the curriculum in the elementary grades, teachers with little knowledge of science or how to teach it could concentrate on subjects like language arts and mathematics that they felt they could teach effectively.

Letting individual teachers choose what science topics to teach resulted in wide variation in the experiences of the children going through the Cabot schools: a few learned a great deal of science; others learned very little; still others were taught selected science topics in several different grades and were never exposed to other topics.

Rose Campion, savvy with an engaging smile and an ability to laugh even when events turn sour, has been superintendent in Cabot for 11 years. This is a long time to be a superintendent in one district. Campion has achieved that tenure by knowing her community: people who pay for and expect a first-rate public school system. As part of a strategy to maintain standards, she periodically commissions reviews of the district's curriculum.

In 1989 Campion asked the district's director of curriculum and instruction, Judy Watson, to establish a committee to review the science curriculum and to produce curricular objectives for kindergarten through grade 12. Recognizing the importance of having different constituencies represented on a committee that would establish curricular goals, Watson put together a Science Curriculum Review Committee consisting of seven teachers, three parents, and one local representative of an environmental group. After two years of reading national reform reports, surveying teachers and parents, and consulting outside experts, the committee produced a plan stipulating that one life science unit and one physical science unit would be part of the core curriculum in each elementary grade.

The science curriculum in grades K through five already included a life science unit; for example, the third grade studied insects, and the fifth grade studied the human body's systems. Implementing the new life science curriculum typically involved supplementing units already in place, including writing new curricula, outlining experiments, and providing new teaching materials. These changes were by no means trivial. However, they were modest compared to the challenge involved in launching an entirely new physical science curriculum.

Superintendent Campion knew that the recommendations of the Science Curriculum Review Committee posed new challenges for Cabot's elementary school teachers and that they would need help in meeting them. Her first step was to make the case to the school board that the new science objectives were valuable and that achieving them would take extra resources. The school board authorized the appointment of an elementary school science coordinator, who would play the leading role in helping teachers learn to teach the new science units. To gain support for this position, Judy Watson promised the budget-conscious school board that the new position would be temporary, lasting for only the two or three years it would take to help teachers implement the new science curriculum.

The topic of the new fifth-grade physical science unit was to be the physics of light. The new elementary school science coordinator, Lauren Getz, saw that one strategy for developing support for the new unit was to have fifth-grade teachers play a role in choosing curricular materials and adapting them for use in Cabot. Two fifth-grade teachers who like science, Jerri Waters and Ron Crain, welcomed the opportunity to work on the curriculum. They began with hands-on materials developed in projects supported by the National Science Foundation. Using these materials, the two teachers and the science coordinator spent a week outlining 13 lessons on topics such as how light travels, how it can be refracted, and how colored light can be mixed. The lessons emphasized the problem-solving skills of developing hypotheses, carrying out experiments, analyzing data, and making inferences from the results—the kinds of skills the Sharpshooters used. Because of the limited time available for curriculum development, the teachers were able to develop detailed plans for only three lessons.

The curriculum outline remained no more than that. By the start of the 1992–93 school year, a full-fledged curriculum on light had not been developed. Nor had there been an opportunity to provide fifth-grade teachers with the two types of help they felt they needed: instruction in the physics of light, and help in learning how to teach light to their students. As a result the district made the light unit optional in

1992–93 and hired Jim Benson, chair of the middle-school science department, to design and teach a course on light to the fifth-grade teachers.

THE WRONG KIND OF TRAINING

It was the fall of 1992 in Cabot, Massachusetts. It was 4:00 P.M. on a Tuesday afternoon. Outside the leaves were turning brilliant autumn colors. Inside, Sharon Wright, Susan Seymour, and the other Cabot fifth-grade teachers were sitting in students' desks, taking a class on how to teach the new science unit on light.

Their instructor, Jim Benson, was well qualified to teach the course. He understood the importance of hands-on learning, and he knew that teachers need to understand the subject matter if they are to be comfortable using hands-on methods. Benson, who had taught science education to student teachers at a local university, took this course seriously. He designed it to extend over 10 two-hour sessions, along the lines of a college physics class. He borrowed equipment to make his demonstrations vivid. He worked hard to pack his lectures with critical, up-to-date information on the physics of light.

Despite these well-intentioned efforts, the course, in Sharon Seymour's words, was "a disaster." The reasons are instructive.

The fifth-grade teachers were not required to take Benson's course. Nonetheless, all of them enrolled initially, largely because they recognized the need for help in preparing to teach the light unit. Judy Watson sought to make enrollment attractive in two ways. For a payment of $110, the teachers could obtain three graduate credits for the course at a nearby college, credits that contributed to reaching the next rung on the district's salary scale. Each teacher who completed the class (eight out of 11),[4] received a stipend of $150 from the Cabot Public Schools Foundation, a parent-run foundation used to supplement the school budget.

Jim Benson began the first class with a pretest so that he would know where each teacher was starting from and so that he could measure how much each participant learned. Sharon Wright found the pretest intimidating: "Six pages, and I could not answer one question." Most other teachers also had problems with the test.

Benson found the results unsettling. He learned, for example, that some teachers thought that people can see objects because light comes from the eye. Because of the teachers' very weak knowledge, Benson decided to concentrate on physics theory. He reasoned that if teachers knew no more than their students, they would be in a weak position to answer questions. From his point of view, it was more important for them to learn theory than how to run experiments.

Sitting in the class at the end of a long day, the teachers were frustrated that what they were learning did not relate directly to the problem they faced: using experiments to teach the properties of light to fifth graders. The teachers who already knew something about the subject found the information helpful. But those who didn't found the experience frustrating. Sharon Wright, for example, tried to do a few of the experiments with her children that Jim Benson had demonstrated. "Some of the experiments required multiple extension cords running across the floor in a room with 27 kids. The light bulbs were fragile. I can't tell you how many we broke."

Susan Seymour, a new teacher at Cabot, was disappointed by the lack of a connection with how she could teach the material. "What should we be doing with the kids? How can we motivate them?"

This experience serves as a useful warning to presidents and governors and others who write goals: even in a school district with big advantages, a professional development course did not do what it was supposed to the first time. The participants knew the importance of having children learn through hands-on investigations. Yet their work together was nothing like a model for the way they wanted to work with those children. The product was a solid course on physics, not a course that would help teachers change the way they teach.

During the school year most of the fifth-grade teachers gave up on teaching the unit on light.

GETTING IT RIGHT

In many districts, the plans for a fifth-grade science unit on light would have ended with Jim Benson's course; the few teachers who were comfortable with science would have done some version of the physics curriculum, and the rest would have spent their time on other subjects. As we will see, Cabot eventually did much better than this. But even as Cabot was floundering, promising staff development programs were taking shape in other school districts. None is an exact blueprint, but each provides insights about the design of effective professional development and what it can accomplish.

Pasadena's SEED Program

In 1986 the Pasadena, California, public schools formed a partnership with the California Institute of Technology to improve science teaching in the district's elementary schools. The goal of the Science for Early Education Development (SEED) program was to provide every elementary school child in the district with "hands-on, minds-on" science—the same goal as at Cabot.[5]

Unlike Cabot, Pasadena schools serve primarily low-income, minority children. One-quarter of the district's students have limited proficiency in English. Class size averages 35 students and expenditures per pupil are $4,200—$3,000 less than in Cabot. But Pasadena schools shared one problem with Cabot: the weak science preparation of elementary school teachers. Few Pasadena elementary school teachers knew much science, and almost none taught science using hands-on methods.

SEED originated in a pilot effort begun in 1986 by two Caltech scientists to improve science teaching in a single elementary school. Over the next four years the scientists and teachers in the pilot school worked together to identify and develop instructional materials and to understand the professional development and support teachers need to teach hands-on science successfully. By 1990 the partners felt they had developed a model that would work for the entire district—a model that focused on long-term professional development to help teachers learn to teach four hands-on science modules at each grade level. Each module provided the basis for 8 to 10 weeks of science learning.

In the spring of 1991 the district asked for volunteers among elementary school teachers at each grade level to spend a week at Caltech during the coming summer. Each volunteer was paid $500 for participating in the summer workshop. During the week at Caltech groups of 10 teachers from each grade level worked with a lead teacher who had experience teaching the science unit and with a Caltech scientist. In each workshop, the agenda was to learn how to teach the first two of the four units. Unlike Jim Benson's physics course, these workshops focused on making the teachers comfortable with the hands-on science units they would teach in their classrooms. Working in groups, the teachers did the experiments, with the lead teacher and scientist guiding the inquiry and modeling questioning techniques.

Like Sharon Wright, the Pasadena teachers were most concerned about classroom management—how to set up the experiments, how to encourage children to work together rather than compete, how to ask questions that would prompt them to make inferences from their data, how to provide feedback on journal entries, how to deal with broken light bulbs. The teachers knew that hands-on science could survive in their classrooms only if they learned to address these logistical and pedagogical issues.

After the teachers had taught the first two units in the first half of the school year, they attended a two-day workshop in January aimed at preparing them to teach the third and fourth units. Recognizing that the teachers would need help and support in this new endeavor, science resource teachers visited their classrooms each week during the first year to answer questions and help in organizing and guiding the experiments.

In the summer of 1992 the SEED teachers spent a second week at Caltech, a week of debriefing. Grouped with the same lead teacher and scientist as in the previous summer, they discussed the experiments in the four units: what things had gone well and what had not, what could be done to make the units work better; and how the science could be integrated with the rest of the curriculum. Like Jim Benson, the scientists and lead teachers knew that classroom teachers had to learn more science to guide students' hands-on inquiries. But they also knew that the learning would be impossible until teachers had gained some confidence in their ability to run hands-on experiments. Only when they knew their classes wouldn't dissolve into chaos would they turn to understanding the underlying science. During the 1992–93 school year the volunteer teachers again received periodic visits from resource teachers to support their efforts at teaching the hands-on science units.

While the first set of volunteers was participating in the second summer of workshops, a second set began the first workshops. This process continued for four years, at the end of which all of the district's elementary school teachers had participated in workshops and all were teaching the four hands-on science units.

In the third stage of the SEED program, teachers who had taught the hands-on units at least twice were given the opportunity to participate in study groups exploring ways to improve the teaching of the units or ways to assess what students had learned. Each study group consisted of three to five teachers at a particular grade level, a science resource teacher, and a professional scientist. The focus of the study groups was the work teachers do and the value of learning from one another to improve the teaching of hands-on science. As of 1995, 55 teachers had participated in the study groups.

Now that all of Pasadena's elementary school teachers are teaching the hands-on science units, assessment of what children are learning has become a major concern. Both the district and the Caltech scientists recognize that evidence that the SEED program is making a difference to children's learning will be essential to sustaining the status that SEED has achieved as *the* elementary school science program in Pasadena. The assessment process is still under way, but analysis of the journals in which every Pasadena elementary school child records what she or he has learned shows that children are learning to pursue an inquiry systematically. There is also evidence that the children's attitudes toward science have changed. Science is now not only a major component of the curriculum, but also a favorite subject.

Wells Junior High School: A Professional Development School

In 1990 the teachers in Wells Junior High School voted to form a partnership with the University of Southern Maine aimed at making their school a professional development school (PDS). The professional development school is a relatively recent innovation, designed to prepare college graduates to become teachers while also providing opportunities for experienced teachers to improve their teaching. It is based in part on the model of the teaching hospital, where interns learn the practice of medicine by observing and then working with experienced physicians.[6]

In the Wells partnership, graduate students at the university preparing to teach became interns at Wells Junior High, with the junior high school faculty assuming the primary responsibility for teaching the interns how to teach effectively. A committee of Wells teachers and university faculty designed the internships. Interns participate in the life of the school from opening day until late May. At several points during the school year, each intern's teaching sessions are videotaped and his or her performance extensively analyzed by the intern and the cooperating teacher.

Although the initial aim of the PDS program was to improve the preparation of novice teachers, it also caused the cooperating teachers to reexamine their own teaching. As one commented: "I think the biggest benefit for me was watching somebody else teach and thinking how I might change it. It forced me to really think about teaching." Another commented: "One of the things I like is that it forces me to verbalize my thinking and planning patterns and think twice or three times about what I do. . . . it's a great method of staff development because it helps you reflect on what you're doing as well as reflect on what the interns do."[7] A second benefit is that the program provides a new role and a leadership opportunity for experienced teachers, reducing the isolation that leads many talented teachers to leave the classroom.

The Philadelphia Writing Project

In 1986 the Philadelphia Writing Project (PhilWP) became a site of the National Writing Project, a network of teachers with more than 150 sites in 43 states. PhilWP adheres to principles of the National Writing Project, which include that high-quality professional development takes place over a long period, that teachers themselves should play a leading role in teaching other teachers, that schools and universities should form collaborative relationships to foster educational change, and that teachers of writing must write themselves.[8]

Each summer the Project offers an intensive three-week institute on writing and literacy for about 30 selected teachers. The institutes provide a rare opportunity for elementary, middle, and high school teachers to learn from one another. The overall design of the institute is planned by teacher facilitators who participated in a previous year. In the institute participants explore their assumptions, beliefs, and prior experiences regarding the theory and practice of writing and language learning. They discuss their classroom teaching practices and students' work with one another and with university faculty and explore how changes in teaching practices can promote and support writing and reading for all students. The summer institute also provides opportunities to share strategies for working with colleagues in schools and for publishing writing emanating from the summer's work.

After the summer institute, teacher participants become part of the network of PhilWP teacher-consultants, which provides opportunities to work closely with other teachers during the school year, both within and across schools and on district-sponsored task forces and program initiatives. Many subsequently participate in PhilWP's advanced institutes, which focus on such topics as teacher research, literature and literacy, and issues related to leadership of school reform efforts. During the first eight years of the Project, funds were available to hire substitute teachers, enabling participants to visit one another's classes to observe and implement ways to improve the teaching of writing. At least four times a year, new teacher-consultants meet to discuss strategies they are trying in their classrooms.

To date there has been no comprehensive evaluation of the extent to which the PhilWP has resulted in improved student writing. However, participants report positive changes in their sense of themselves as teachers in an urban school district. For one, the PhilWP institute "was the first place that . . . I found out that . . . having questions and asking questions was really okay. In fact, that it was smart [for a teacher] to have questions." For another, the most valuable part of the Writing Project has been the intellectual component, "the kind of stimulation that I found there." And for yet another, PhilWP "totally shook my thinking and made me see the child first. . . . When I changed my teaching . . . it was just miraculous, the results I saw."

CABOT RECOUPS

On the basis of feedback about Jim Benson's course, the Cabot administration recognized that the district's fifth graders would learn about the physics of light through hands-on, minds-on methods only if the teachers received effective help in learning to teach the unit. With this goal in mind, the district hired David Parnes, a retired science teacher from a neighboring school system who had considerable experience working with elementary school teachers, to work with the fifth-grade teachers.

During the 1993–94 school year, Parnes provided intensive assistance to the teachers who requested his help. For example, he spent 10 Tuesday afternoons with Susan Seymour. First he taught a lesson with her for an hour, modeling how to ask questions that provoke active thinking, such as

"Why did you do that? Could you do it any other way?" He encouraged the children to think about how they could measure the results of their experiments, asking them to think how rulers and protractors might be helpful. After the children had left for the day, Parnes and Seymour discussed how the lesson had gone. As Seymour described it, "We talked about the lesson, about what the different groups were discovering, where they were, where they should be." Then they discussed how Seymour should conduct her lesson on Thursday, building on the students' Tuesday work.

Susan Seymour felt that David Parnes's help would have a lasting effect on her science teaching. She also felt that with Parnes's help, the light unit was an important experience for many of the children in her class. "It is the kids challenging the kids, and that is pretty exciting."

Cabot's teachers learned not only from David Parnes but also from one another. Some elementary school teachers formed teams to help one another organize the science lessons and assemble the equipment. In grade-level meetings, they discussed how they could modify experiments to make them work better.

Support from Cabot's administration made these interactions possible, if not easy. Principals authorized teachers to work together in supervising science experiments for some groups of children while aides worked with other children. Every Wednesday the school day for children ends at 12:15, leaving the afternoon for planning and collaboration. While the Cabot teachers are quick to point out that the Wednesday afternoons quickly become fully booked, and grade-level meetings take place only four times a year, the Cabot schedule provides more opportunities for collaboration than do schedules in most public school districts.

PROFESSIONAL DEVELOPMENT THAT WORKS

The staff development programs described in this chapter differ from each other in important respects. Put differently, there is no single recipe for successful professional development. Each school must find a way of enhancing teachers' skills that is consistent with its own strategy for implementing the Five Principles.

At the same time, the programs share common characteristics that bear restating. In every case, the professional development effort is part of a strategy for accomplishing clearly defined goals. All focus on the core activity of schooling: how teachers teach on a day-to-day basis. All provide opportunities for participation and—the scarcest resource in schools—time for learning. All of the programs are long-term efforts: they implicitly recognize that classroom management issues dominate the first year of any serious change effort. All provide access to outside expertise, with university faculty seen as partners, not superiors, of the classroom teachers.

The characteristics of promising professional development efforts look very much like the characteristics of quality circles at good firms: frontline workers learning from one another to solve the problems of daily work, with access to outside expertise and support for problem-solving activities. As is the case with training in best-practice firms, the successful professional development efforts are part of strategies to implement the Five Principles.

The one principle that each of the change efforts described in this chapter is still struggling to implement is measuring progress. Managements in Cabot, Pasadena, Wells, and Philadelphia recognize that this Fourth Principle is important: continued funding for promising professional development efforts depends on evidence that they make a difference to student learning. Each district is working to find ways of assessing whether their professional development efforts are resulting in better student skills. The assessment task is difficult because the change efforts focus on helping children to acquire skills that are not easily measured on conventional multiple-choice tests. The next chapter focuses on efforts to improve measures of student progress in mastering the New Basic Skills—a challenge every district faces.

Creating an environment that supports the continued learning of frontline workers is expensive, but it is not a frill. It is the way to improve the quality of learning. Increasing the number of children who master the New Basic Skills will take as great a long-term commitment to developing the skills of the nation's teachers as Northwestern Mutual Life, Honda, and other best-practice firms make in developing the skills of their work forces.

CHAPTER 7

THE FOURTH PRINCIPLE
MEASURE PROGRESS REGULARLY

The Sharpshooters took almost a year to solve the stopped-blower-nut problem. But in the end they presented convincing evidence that they had done so, and that the solution contributed to Honda's goal of improving quality. Defining a clear goal and measuring progress toward the goal are parts of the design of every quality circle at HAM.

It took seven years for Northwestern Mutual Life to fully implement Workbench, and the first years were full of setbacks. But NML persevered with Workbench in part because the firm had good indicators of service quality, and management knew that it would be able to document the positive effects on that quality when they were realized. For HAM, NML, and other best-practice firms, the ability to monitor progress toward organizational goals is critical to maintaining support for expensive long-term investments and innovations that contribute to service quality.

In the absence of reliable information about progress toward its goals, an organization has no way to distinguish successful policies from failures. The problem is especially difficult for schools trying to teach the New Basic Skills. The usual means of measuring student skills are standardized, multiple-choice tests. These tests are fine at measuring skills like the ability to do long division or fractions. But they are ineffective in measuring how well a student structures a problem or clearly communicates the solution.

CAMP PORTFOLIO

In June 1994, 125 fourth- and eighth-grade teachers from Vermont public schools arrived at Johnson State College, 40 miles north of Ben and Jerry's ice cream factory, to spend five days at "Camp Portfolio." As at most camps, the first day was devoted to orientation. But orientation did not involve pointing out the swimming pool and volleyball courts. Instead, the teachers practiced scoring the mathematics and writing work of Vermont fourth- and eighth-graders to develop skill in grading with common standards. The 30 teachers scoring the mathematics work of fourth graders spent the first day evaluating responses to problems like the Magic Rings.

The Magic Rings problem differs from the simple computation problems typically included on tests of U.S. elementary school children's mathematics skills—and on the test taken by applicants for $6.35-an-hour jobs as pickers at Sports Plus. Instead of requiring only computations, solving the Magic Rings problem requires figuring out what is asked and designing an analysis strategy—a lot to ask of a fourth-grader, but much closer to the New Basic Skills required for success in today's economy than computational speed and accuracy.

The method of scoring the Magic Rings problem also differed from that used for conventional tests. Instead of determining simply whether the child wrote down the correct

Magic Rings

It's your birthday. You have just turned 9 years old. Your present is three boxes of magic rings. The instruction book that goes with the rings says:

- You can wear no more than ten rings at a time.
- Once a ring is worn, it loses its power.

Contents: 10 rings	Contents: 10 rings	Contents: 10 rings
Blue Rings	**Green Rings**	**Yellow Rings**
Each blue ring doubles your age.	Each green ring adds 5 years to your age.	Each yellow ring takes 2 years away from your age.

You put some rings on your fingers and start to grow at once. Within seconds, the magic works and you are 40 years old. Your two friends, also fourth graders, do the same thing. All of you are now 40 years old.

Which rings are each of you wearing?

Before you begin working, take some time to think about the problem and how you will come up with a solution. *Because there are lots of different ways these friends could wear the rings, you won't be able to find all of them in the time allowed. Show as many as you think you need to support your solution.*

Show all of your work, including scratch work, and write your complete solution in the response booklet. You can put charts, tables, graphs or drawings on the lined pages or on the dot page.

In your solution be sure to include the following:

- Factors you thought might affect the solution to the problem
- How you solved the problem
- Reasons for decisions you made along the way
- Anything you discovered as you solved the problem
- Accurate, appropriate mathematical language
- Accurate, appropriate representation

Then check . . .

- Did I answer the question?
- Will someone who reads my solution know how I solved this problem and the reasons for my decisions?

Figure 7.1: 1994 Vermont Uniform Assessment Mathematics Part 2: Problem Grade 4

Adapted from a *Balanced Assessment Task. Balanced Assessment* is a National Science Foundation Project.

answer, the teachers at Camp Portfolio evaluated the quality of his or her work in seven dimensions. In each dimension, the teacher assigned a grade ranging from 1 to 4 on the basis of standards described in a rating scale (Table 7.1). Figure 7.2 reproduces one of the responses that the teachers were asked to evaluate.

After considerable debate, the fourth-grade teachers agreed with Jill Rosenblum, the leader of the group and one of the committee that had assigned the benchmark grades, on the appropriate scores for the student answer. The response merited a grade of 3 for understanding the problem (PS1), developing an approach (PS2), and showing work that suggested appropriate reasoning for solving the problem (PS3). The grade for "so what" (PS4) was 2, reflecting the judgment that this child demonstrated the ability to make observations. The score was not a 3 because the child, like most in Vermont public schools, had not developed significant skill in forming generalizations from particular problems. The grades for mathematical language (C1) and presentation (C3) were 3, reflecting consistent use of arithmetic terms, inclusion of a running total, and a relatively clear presentation. The grade for mathematical presentation (C2) was 1, reflecting the lack of diagrams, charts, tables, or drawings in the answer. Scoring the quality of presentation reflects the concern of Vermont educators that children learn not only to solve problems but also to communicate their problem-solving strategies clearly. Honda of America expected the same from the Sharpshooters.

Throughout their first day at Camp Portfolio the teachers argued, often heatedly, about their evaluations of students' work. The discussions focused on what constitute good

Table 7.1

Mathematics Problem-Solving and Communication Criteria, Fourth-Grade Math Portfolio

	Rating				Rating
	Level 1	Level 2	Level 3	Level 4	
PS1 Understanding the Problem	. . . didn't understand enough to get started or make progress.	. . . understood enough to solve part of the problem or to get part of a solution.	. . . understood the problem.	. . . identifies special factors that influenced the approach before starting the problem.	
PS2 How Student Solved the Problem	. . . approach didn't work.	. . . approach would only lead to solving part of the problem.	. . . approach would work for the problem.	. . . approach was efficient or sophisticated.	
PS3 Why—Decisions Along the Way	. . . no reasoning is evident from the work or reasoning is incorrect.	. . . only partly correct reasoning or correct reasoning used for only part of the problem.	. . . didn't clearly explain reasons for decisions, but work suggests correct reasoning used throughout the problem.	. . . clearly explained the reasons for the correct decisions made throughout the problem.	
PS4 So What— Outcomes of Activities	. . . solved the problem and stopped.	. . . solved the problem and made comments about something in the solution.	. . . solved the problem and connected the solution to other math OR described a use for what was learned in the "real world."	. . . solved the problem and made a general rule about the solution or extended the solution to a more complicated situation.	

C1 Mathematical Language	. . . didn't use any math vocabulary, equations, or notations, or used them incorrectly.	. . . used basic math words or basic math notation correctly.	. . . went beyond occasional use of basic math language and used the language correctly.	. . . relied heavily on sophisticated math language to communicate the solution.
C2 Mathematical Representation	. . . didn't use any graphs, tables, charts, models, diagrams, or drawings to communicate the solution.	. . . attempted to use appropriate representation.	. . . used appropriate math representation accurately and appropriately.	. . . used sophisticated graphs, tables, charts, models, diagrams, or drawings to communicate the solution.
C3 Presentation	. . . response is unclear.	. . . response contains some clear parts.	. . . if others read this response, they would have to fill in some details to understand the solution.	. . . response is well organized and detailed.

communication and problem-solving skills, how first-rate work differs from less adequate work, and what types of problems elicit the best work. In essence, the discussions were about standards.

The remaining days at Camp Portfolio were spent scoring the writing and mathematics work in the portfolios of approximately 2,000 fourth- and eighth-graders chosen ran-

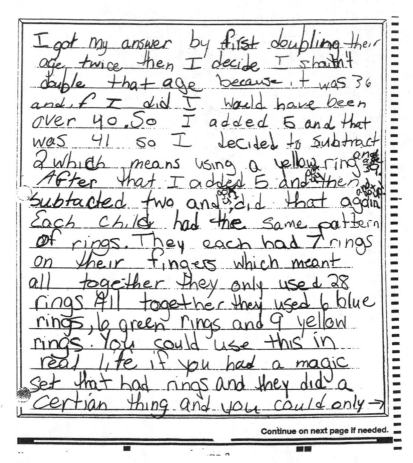

I got my answer by first doubling their age, twice then I decide I shouldn't double that age because it was 36 and if I did I would have been over 40. So I added 5 and that was 41 so I decided to subtract 2 which means using a yellow ring. After that I added 5 and then subtacted two and did that again. Each child had the same pattern of rings. They each had 7 rings on their fingers which meant all together they only used 28 rings. All together they used 6 blue rings, 6 green rings and 9 yellow rings. You could use this in real life if you had a magic set that had rings and they did a certian thing and you could only →

Continue on next page if needed.

Figure 7.2: A Vermont Fourth-Grader's Answer to the Magic Rings Problem

domly from Vermont's 60 supervisory unions (geographic groupings of small school districts; each union has a superintendent). Each portfolio consisted of five to seven pieces of writing or mathematics work from the preceding school year.

MATHEMATICS: PART 2 (continued)   03893

Be sure to show all of your work, including scratch work.

use so many of them!

Continue on next page if needed.

PLEASE DO NOT WRITE IN THIS AREA

Figure 7.2: *Continued*

MATHEMATICS: PART 2 (continued) *03893*

You may use this page to continue your work or for a table, chart, graph or drawing. Be sure to show all of your work, including scratch work.

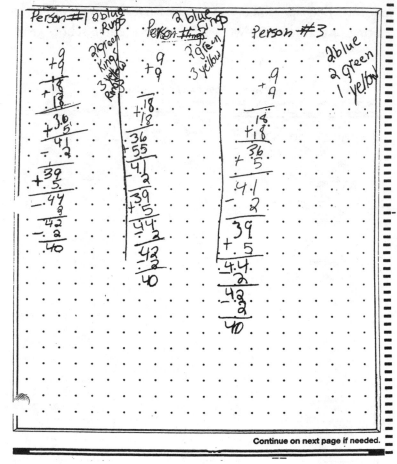

Continue on next page if needed.

Figure 7.2: *Continued*

Why did the teachers come to Camp Portfolio? Not because it was a vacation; they started scoring at 8:45 A.M. and finished at suppertime on the short days, at 9:00 P.M. on the longer days. Not because the accommodations were luxurious; they slept two or three to a room in spartan dormitories and made their own beds. The $500 each participant received for the five days, a significant supplement to modest Vermont teacher salaries, was an incentive. Most came, however, because it was a chance to talk with colleagues teaching the same subjects, to collect new problems to use in their classrooms, to see the work of other Vermont schoolchildren, to get new ideas, and to develop more skill in evaluating how their own students' work measured up to the state standards. In the words of Deborah Armitrage, a fourth-grade teacher from a rural district in northeast Vermont, "Through the scoring I find my own personal weaknesses in what I am doing with my children. By seeing so many portfolios and listening to Jill [Rosenblum] I find lots . . . that I can bring back to my children."

Given the generally dismal record of professional development for teachers, the discussions at Camp Portfolio were remarkable. They focused on the quality of student work as measured against external standards concerning the extent to which students had mastered critical elements of the New Basic Skills.

Camp Portfolio is part of a Vermont Department of Education program to provide citizens and businesses with information about the skills of the state's schoolchildren. The children's scores serve as part of the basis for two reports each fall by the Department of Education. The first report describes the quality of Vermont fourth- and eighth-graders' work in seven dimensions for mathematics and five for writing and compares the scores to those of the previous year. For example, the 1993 report showed that Vermont eighth-graders were quite good at understanding problems, at selecting an effective strategy for solution, and at making a clear presentation of the results. Their greatest weaknesses were seeing connections among important math concepts and connections between the math they do in class and its use in the world outside the classroom.[1] This report provides detailed information about the extent to which Vermont students are learning to solve problems and to communicate clearly—both critical aspects of the New Basic Skills.

The second report provides information on mathematics proficiency of fourth- and eighth-graders in each supervisory union—information that parents, taxpayers, and businesses can use in evaluating the adequacy of public education, and that teachers and principals can use to improve teaching and learning.[2] Together, the reports provide information about the progress Vermont schools are making toward critical educational goals. An indication of employers' interest in this initiative is that the Vermont Business Roundtable has made small grants to school districts to hold "School Report Nights," at which school officials explain to their communities the data on local children's assessment scores.

Vermont is not the only place where educators are experimenting with new strategies for assessing mastery of the New Basic Skills. Since 1987 Pittsburgh, Pennsylvania, has used portfolios to provide teachers, parents, and taxpayers with information about the writing skills of children in the city's public schools.[3] Students attending Central Park East Secondary School in East Harlem qualify for graduation by presenting to a committee of reviewers essays, projects, and videotaped performances that illustrate the work they have done and the skills and knowledge they have acquired.[4] Kentucky uses student portfolios as part of its recently enacted educational accountability system. The story of how student portfolios came to Vermont and what the program has

meant for public education there demonstrates the importance of the Fourth Principle—the need to measure organizational performance.

HOW PORTFOLIO ASSESSMENT
CAME TO VERMONT

Until the late 1980s no chronicler of educational reform
would have devoted much attention to Vermont. Local control has always been important in the state, and each of Vermont's 279 school districts values its independence. In contrast to its western neighbor, New York, with its
century-long tradition of an activist state department of education, the Vermont Department of Education, located on
two floors of the modest-sized State Office Building across
from the capitol, historically has not been a potent force
pushing for changes in local educational practices.

During the 1980s this situation began to change. Madeline
Kunin, the reform-minded governor, convinced the legislature
to double the amount of state aid provided to local school districts. The need to defend the accompanying tax increase led
legislators to ask, What is the money buying? The governor's
response was that the money would buy better education.

Ross Brewer, the director of planning and policy development for the Department of Education from 1983 to 1993,
played a key role in developing the portfolio assessment system. A jovial ex-academic who decided that staying in Vermont provided a better life than academic tenure elsewhere,
Brewer described his position as the best job in state government—despite the fact that his hair turned prematurely gray
during his years there. He described the need to develop an

accountability system: "Madeline would say [to educators], 'We're going to give you lots more, but then we're going to come back to you and ask you what we got for our money.' . . . the governor was very interested in pointing out to people that accountability was going to be part of this."

In 1987, Richard P. Mills left New Jersey, where he had served as Governor Thomas Kean's liaison to other states on educational reform issues, to become Vermont's commissioner of education. Deeply committed to improving education in Vermont, Mills knew that the mandate to develop an accountability system was both an opportunity and a danger. The opportunity came from the potential to affect teaching and learning. Mills knew that the states and the federal government had tried a wide variety of strategies—including new curricula, compensatory education, training for teachers, team teaching, and open classrooms—to improve the nation's schools. Many of these reform efforts had evoked creative responses from some teachers, but none had led to widespread, sustained changes in what teachers and children do in classrooms. An exception has been accountability systems. Using student scores on prescribed tests to make judgments about the quality of education provided in particular schools or school districts has evoked changes in what happens in classrooms. Thus the mandate to develop an accountability system seemed to provide an opportunity to improve the quality of public education in Vermont.

The danger came from evidence that to date teachers' responses to the types of tests used in accountability systems had not increased the likelihood that students mastered the New Basic Skills. For example, the National Science Board attributes the decline in American students' problem-solving skills during the 1980s to the increased use of minimum competency tests for determining eligibility for promotions and high school graduation. The testing led teachers to focus instruction on the computational skills that were given great weight on the test, and to neglect problem-solving skills because they received little weight on the tests.[5] Students' computational skills did rise during the 1980s, but these skills are not enough to obtain access to a middle-class job today.

Mills wanted to design an accountability system that would improve teaching. He began by talking with Vermonters concerned with public education. During 1988 Mills and Ross Brewer invited superintendents, principals, teachers, school board members, and employers to a number of dinners to discuss the design of an accountability system. Brewer described a scenario that occurred at every dinner:

> At each of these meetings we asked people, Do you do standardized testing? And everybody did standardized testing. Now, there's no state testing program, so it wasn't the state. . . . And so we'd ask teachers, . . . How do you use the information? And they would say, we don't. And so we would say, well then why do you do it? And they'd say, because the principal makes us. So then we turn to the . . . two or three principals at this meeting and say, why do you do standardized testing, why do you make the teachers do it? They say it upsets their classes. . . . it doesn't give them information they use. Well, we do it because the superintendent thinks we ought to. So then you turn to the . . . superintendents . . . and say, well, the principal doesn't use the information and the teacher doesn't use the information, so why are you using standardized testing? Well, because the community expects it. So then you turn to a board member and say, well, the superintendent doesn't really use the information, the principal doesn't use the information, the teacher doesn't use the information, everybody's doing standardized testing, why do they do it? Well, we don't know.

> The superintendent comes in once a year, gives us a half-hour report, tells us our kids are above average and that things are okay. So everybody was doing standardized testing, [but] nobody knew why they were doing it.

These discussions also made clear that teachers disliked the tests. Because the tests were not closely related to the schools' instructional goals, children's scores did not provide a fair assessment either of their mastery of what they had been taught or of the quality of teaching. Moreover, time spent taking the tests reduced instruction time.

Employers at these meetings voiced concerns about the skills of high school graduates. Because of the very low unemployment rate in Vermont, employers were sometimes forced to hire graduates who did not write well or did not have good problem-solving skills. They also found it difficult to get information from the schools about students' academic performances.

These many conversations with groups concerned about Vermont public education led Mills and Brewer to conclude that the state needed new methods of assessing students' skills. Accordingly, in October 1988 Mills recommended to the State Board of Education the development of a new system of measuring student performance, based in part on portfolios containing students' best work from the preceding school year. One goal of the system was to respond to the legislature's desire for accountability measures. But, as Mills explained to the Board of Education and the legislature, there were also several other goals, including avoiding the distortions of educational practice that conventional test-based accountability induced, encouraging good teaching, providing a focus for professional development, and providing high standards for student work.

Mills made clear that the development of new methods of student performance would be an expensive and time-consuming process. As Brewer put it, "There are no smart people to copy on this one." It was nevertheless a useful investment, they argued, because the new assessments would not only provide better information about the skills of Vermont students; more important, they would be a vehicle for improving public education in the state. The Board of Education approved the proposal and initiated five years of intense activity involving large numbers of Vermont educators.

DEVELOPING THE NEW ASSESSMENT SYSTEM

Early in the discussions about developing a new assessment system, Mills and Brewer decided that it should focus on writing and mathematics. The attraction of writing was that most schools in the state had already introduced "process writing," an approach that emphasized multiple drafts and peer criticism of early drafts. Implementation of the process-writing curriculum had necessitated determining the goals of writing and the appropriate standards for judging it—both issues critical to the development of new assessment strategies. Mills and Brewer were also aware that the National Council of Teachers of Mathematics (NCTM) was about to publish a report describing the mathematical skills American children should have at each grade level, and providing examples of problems they should be able to solve to demonstrate those skills.[6] This report would give Vermont educators a framework for setting goals for students' mathematical skills and ways of assessing these skills.

Initially Mills planned to develop statewide assessments for fourth-, eighth-, and eleventh-graders, but on the advice of a panel of employers appointed by the Vermont Business Roundtable, he decided to focus first on the two lower grades and later phase in the eleventh-grade assessment.

From the beginning, teachers liked the idea that portfolios would play a central role in the new assessment system. The process of building portfolios seemed likely to promote both good teaching and classroom dialogue about standards for good work. The requirement that portfolios include multiple drafts of writing products would encourage children to revise work and to learn to appreciate the value of persevering with projects to improve the products. Asking children to evaluate each other's work and to explain their own approaches would help them to develop communication skills and to learn to work productively in groups. These are all elements of the New Basic Skills.

Once the commitment was made to an assessment system in which portfolios of student work would play a major role, a host of practical questions arose: Must the writing portfolios include examples of specific types of writing, such as letters or essays? Must the mathematics portfolios for a particular grade level include students' solutions to the same problems? What criteria would be used for assessing the quality of work in each area? What should the scoring system be? Who would do the scoring? Who would have access to the assessment scores—parents? employers? taxpayers? Answers to these and many other questions had to be found in the process of developing and implementing the new system.

Decisions about the practical workings of the assessment system were complicated by the advice of experts on assessment, who pointed out that a design that would best fulfill the objective of improving teaching would be quite different from a design that would provide the most reliable evidence about children's skills. To stimulate good classroom discussions about standards for good writing, teachers had to be free to choose topics for writing assignments that interested them and their students. As a result, essays in the writing portfolios would deal with different topics and it would be difficult to score these essays in a consistent manner. Requiring all students to write about the same topic would probably result in more reliable scoring, but this would also reduce teachers' discretion in organizing instruction.

Recognizing that the new assessment system would be a success only if teachers supported it, Mills decided to have them play a central role in the design of the system. In Ross Brewer's words: "From the very beginning our commitment was, it's got to be teachers who do this because they're the ones who come out of the classroom, and they're the ones who know what the challenges are. . . . If the Department [of Education] had come in, or if we had brought experts up from Harvard, the thing would have gone right down the tube. . . . It wouldn't have had any credibility, and probably wouldn't have resonated with what teachers really needed."

The committees of teachers chosen to design the assessment system faced a near-herculean task: all were skilled teachers, but none had extensive backgrounds in testing and measurement. Nevertheless, both the mathematics and writing committees produced operational plans for an assessment system in time for piloting in the 1991–92 school year.[7] The mathematics assessment was composed of three parts: five to seven best pieces of student work, whole portfolios of student work, and student responses to a mathematics examination administered statewide to all students in a particular grade. The goal of the "best pieces" part of the assessment was to assess problem-solving abilities and communication skills. The whole portfolios of student work would provide a picture of the work done throughout the school year. The scores on the uniform test would indicate understanding of particular concepts and could link the performance of Vermont students with those of students in other states. Teachers were asked to include among the students' best pieces work on puzzles, applications, and investigations. The *Teacher's Guide* explained that puzzles are tasks that require students to identify and explore approaches to nonroutine problems, applications require students to apply knowledge they already possess, and investigations include explorations and analysis that leads to conclusions.[8] Although the *Teacher's Guide* provided examples of each type of task, teachers were free to find or devise the tasks that their students worked on for their portfolios.

In addition to determining the composition of the assessment, teachers also developed "rubrics," procedures for scoring student work. Instead of giving each of the "best pieces" a single grade, they developed a multidimensional scoring system designed to provide detailed information about strengths and weaknesses. Each piece submitted would be graded in the seven dimensions described in Figure 7.2, four of which related to problem solving and three to communication. The grades on a particular dimension would be averaged among the best pieces, producing a total of seven grades, one for each dimension. The committee decided not to average scores across dimensions because doing this would reduce the quality of the information provided by the assessment. For example, a student might devise a clever analytic strategy but communicate it poorly. Averaging a high score with a low score would conceal both important strengths and significant weaknesses.

This focus on acquiring detailed information about many dimensions of performance harkens back to NML's and Honda's implementation of the Fourth Principle. These firms were not satisfied with one or two measures of performance, such as quarterly profits or total sales. They recognized that a thorough understanding of the health of their organizations and the ability to pinpoint areas of weakness required a rich array of performance measures.

PROFESSIONAL DEVELOPMENT: THE THIRD PRINCIPLE

It soon became clear that the emphasis on problem solving and communication in the new mathematics assessments would require significant changes in the practices of most teachers. Typical instructional strategies—teacher explanations followed by student completion of worksheets and exercises in the back of mathematics textbooks—would not develop the problem-solving and communications skills that were central in the new assessment system. Teachers would need considerable long-term help to change those strategies.

One of the first people to point out the need for ongoing help was Jill Rosenblum, a fourth-grade math teacher in Stratford, whose school participated in the piloting of the new assessment system. Ross Brewer found Rosenblum's complaints compelling and was impressed by her ideas. He persuaded her to leave her teaching position and to design a system of ongoing professional development to improve the mathematics teaching of the state's fourth- and eighth-grade teachers.

The system of professional development designed by Jill Rosenblum and her colleagues is based on the idea of a network. Each school is part of one of 17 networks, and the fourth- and eighth-grade teachers in each network meet for training four times a year. Most networks have four leaders, one for each subject for each grade in which the assessment take place. The network leaders not only lead the training session, but also provide ongoing support to the teachers in their network. As Rosenblum describes the system: "I am the trainer's trainer, and the trainers themselves are all classroom teachers, and that was the design, to take classroom practitioners who were having some success, give them more tools to have more success, give them training and professional development, and then [have them] lead a series of local meetings to provide training to their colleagues." The network training is supplemented by summer institutes which provide Vermont teachers with opportunities to explore in depth strategies for teaching effectively with portfolios.

HIGH STAKES OR LOW STAKES?

Measuring progress often leads directly to the question: How will the measurements be used? In the case of Underwriter's Workbench, it was clear that NML managers would track the productivity of underwriters using the new system and use the measurements to determine whether the project should continue. Vermont faced a more complicated decision about the use of portfolio scores. At one extreme was the possibility of devising high-stakes consequences, perhaps making teachers' salaries or even their jobs depend on the results. At the other extreme was the possibility of not reporting results for particular school districts at all. Mills and Brewer rejected both strategies. They recognized that high-stakes consequences would alienate teachers and jeopardize their most important goal, improving teaching in Vermont's public schools. On the other hand, if the Department of Education did not publish information on the performances of children by school district, the legislature and the Business Roundtable would probably withdraw support of the new assessment system, which they saw as promoting accountability.

As a middle-ground strategy, Mills and Brewer proposed that the Department of Education provide each community with a report describing the distribution of scores for the students in their public schools. The report would begin with a description of the community, its schools, and its students. Information about the community would include household income, educational attainments of adult residents, and property values. School data would include per-student spending, student-teacher ratios, and the percentage of faculty participating in assessment-related professional development activities. Similarly, student data would include the percentages of students in special education, compensatory education, and preschool programs. Every table would include not only information about the community, its schools, or its students but also analogous information for the state as a whole. The purpose was to provide readers with a basis for judging how the community compared to the state. For example, residents in a relatively affluent, well-educated community that spent an above-average amount of money on public schools would be primed to expect relatively high scores for students in their schools.[9]

The report would then provide results on the distribution of portfolio assessment scores for the community's students. The data would include separate distributions of scores for each of the seven dimensions in which mathematics portfolios were graded and the five dimensions in which writing portfolios were graded. To facilitate comparison, the same information would be provided for the state as a whole, and for a sample of similar communities in the state.

Would these community reports be a low-stakes or a high-stakes use of the assessment scores? The answer would depend on the responses of residents. If they were not interested in the results, the stakes would be low. If their response was to demand dramatic changes in the schools, the stakes could be quite high. In typical Vermont fashion, Mills and Brewer saw their job not as determining what the stakes should be, but as providing communities with good information and letting the communities decide how to use it.

RELIABILITY OF THE PORTFOLIO SCORING

Developing and maintaining a system of performance indicators that provides useful information is a challenge for every organization. NML, Honda, and other best-practice firms must evaluate periodically whether the performance indicators they collect provide management with the information needed to make good decisions. Like these firms, Vermont faced difficult issues in the design of its system of performance indicators.

Not only do most school districts in Vermont have only one elementary school; a great many have only one fourth-grade class and one eighth-grade class. Consequently, reporting portfolio scores by school district means reporting the scores of the students who worked with individual teachers. Understandably this has been a concern for many Vermont teachers. Some teachers fear that students' scores might reflect the grading practices of individual scorers more than they reflected the skills of their students. To allay these fears, Mills agreed that no scores would be reported by school district until there was evidence that the teachers doing the scoring had succeeded in adopting quite uniform grading standards—in technical terms, until interrater reliability was high.

To determine the reliability of the portfolio scoring, Mills asked the Rand Corporation, a nationally respected research firm, to conduct an independent review of the Vermont portfolio assessment system and to examine the reliability of scores from teachers' ratings of students' mathematics and writing portfolios. The Rand group found that in the first year of the program different teachers scored the same student mathematics and writing portfolios quite differently. As a result, there was a good chance that differences in students' scores reflected differences in grading practices rather than differences in the quality of work.[10]

Several factors contributed to the low reliability of the first-year scoring. First, the decision to rate each best mathematics piece in seven dimensions and each best writing piece in five dimensions (as opposed to giving an overall rating) required teachers to draw quite subtle inferences about the weaknesses of individual pieces of work. Although in theory the dimensions differed, in practice they often blurred together.

The rapid pace at which the portfolio program was introduced also contributed to the low reliability of the scoring. Most of the professional development activities in preparation for the first year of statewide implementation focused on using portfolios in teaching. While most fourth- and eighth-grade teachers participated in workshops dealing with scoring portfolios, these were held shortly before the statewide scoring in April. This timing provided few opportunities for teachers to discuss scoring procedures with colleagues and to reassess the standards appropriate for assigning particular scores.

Mills recognized the importance of the reliability issue and agreed not to publish scores pertaining to individual districts until the Rand research showed that the reliabilities had increased. In the fall of 1992 he hired Sue Rigney, who had just developed a new mathematics test for use in Michigan's statewide assessment program, to be director of assessment for the Vermont Department of Education. This appointment demonstrated Mill's recognition that changes in the assessment system were needed to meet the goal of providing meaningful information about academic performance in individual school districts.

Acting in part on advice from the Rand analysts, Sue Rigney and her colleagues implemented a number of changes in the assessment system to increase the reliability of scoring. First, whereas scoring in the first year had been done at six regional centers by volunteer teachers, in the second year all scoring was done at a single site to facilitate common training. Second, teachers were given immediate feedback about the extent to which their scoring matched benchmark scores provided by network leaders. Third, the uniform mathematics test was redesigned to include a single open-ended problem tackled by all Vermont fourth-graders (and a different problem for all eighth-graders) in addition to 30 multiple-choice items drawn from a national test. (The Magic Rings was the common problem in the fourth-grade assessment for 1994.) Finally, students were no longer to include puzzles among their best pieces because puzzles were unlikely to provide good opportunities to display the full range of problem-solving and communication skills included in the scoring system.

Coupled with greater experience in scoring, these changes led to significant improvements in the reliability of the math scoring.[11] The Rand Corporation concluded that the reliability of the mathematics scoring for the second year was sufficiently high to justify reporting information on the math scores for Vermont's 60 supervisory unions. Beginning in January 1994, information on the quality of the mathematics portfolios for fourth- and eighth-graders in individual supervisory unions has been included in the annual *Condition of Education in Vermont* report.

Progress in improving the reliability of the writing scoring was slower. For a second year, the reliabilities remained too low to justify reporting scores on writing portfolios for supervisory unions. The state report on writing only compared scores for the state as a whole for the 1992–93 school year with scores in the previous year.

Although the problem of scoring students' writing reliably remains a problem, evidence from the Pittsburgh school district, which has been using writing portfolios since 1987, indicates that it is not intractable. There teachers trained in scoring were able to grade three dimensions of students' writing portfolios with very little variation in scores across raters. The resulting reliabilities were high enough to justify public reporting of scores by school and would have been so in Vermont as well. Learning from Pittsburgh, Mills, Rigney, and the small group overseeing portfolio assessment in Vermont are considering both additional training for scorers and reduction of the number of dimensions in which portfolios are scored.

Vermont's struggle to improve the reliability of the portfolio scoring makes it easy to understand why so many school districts stick with multiple-choice tests as measures of student skills even if they don't capture important dimensions of the New Basic Skills. But Vermont educators recognized that the effort to encourage the development of communication and problem-solving skills in the state's classrooms could succeed only if the performance measures assessed these skills. Thus, in persevering with portfolio assessment, Vermont educators are trying to avoid the mistake of the Russian nails described in Chapter 5, where the incentives that Moscow provided to the nail factory in Smirsk—make 10 metric tons of nails—were inconsistent with the real goals—produce a large number of nails of many different sizes. In other words, the Vermont educators are trying to get the incentives right. A glimpse at the responses in one community illustrates the progress that has been made.

PORTFOLIO ASSESSMENT
IN FRANKLIN NORTHWEST

The Franklin Northwest Supervisory Union is located in the northwestern corner of Vermont. Primarily agricultural with almost no industrial base, it is one of the lowest-income regions of the state and has the lowest per-student expenditures of the 60 supervisory unions. The three rooms that constitute the central office are located in the back of a two-story 85-year-old brick building across from the town green in Swanton, population 5,400. To reach the superintendent's office, one must walk through the town clerk's office.

Doug Harris, the superintendent of Franklin Northwest, is an enthusiastic supporter of portfolio assessment. Although his reactions to the portfolio initiative and those of the principals and teachers of Franklin Northwest are not shared by all Vermont educators, they do illustrate how portfolio assessment can affect teaching and learning. They also point out some of the issues that arise with its implementation.

For Doug Harris, there is little question that portfolio assessment is changing the way teaching and learning are taking place in the schools of Franklin Northwest: "I see differences in the kind of work that kids do. I see differences when I walk in a classroom. . . . there's a difference in the way [kids] can talk about what they're doing."

One way Doug Harris has supported portfolio assessment is to find money to pay for substitutes so that teachers can attend network training. He has also supported teachers' request to design and implement their own course on how to use portfolios to improve instruction and assessment.

Highgate Elementary School is one of three schools in the supervisory union with fourth grades. For Brian DuPrat, a former high school mathematics teacher who is the principal of Highgate, portfolio assessment is "the Trojan horse of changing instruction." He sees it as primarily responsible for dramatic changes in fourth-grade mathematics instruction: "the assessment process . . . really stretched the [fourth grade] team to reexamine their teaching of mathematics, and we have quite literally gone from a drill-and-practice sort of curriculum to a very hands-on, experiential type of mathematics, much more in alignment with the assessment practice."

JoAnne Campbell and Faith Johnson, two veteran fourth-grade teachers at Highgate, have worked together to change the way they teach mathematics. Both feel that their attempts to prepare their students for the mathematics assessment have changed their teaching. JoAnne Campbell:

You're not just looking at the back of the math book and doing the basic word problems anymore. You're constantly looking beyond and looking for more challenging examples. . . . In math especially, I work on teaching the children more strategies for solving different types of problems, logical reasoning, finding a pattern, working backwards, guess and check—a variety of different ways to approach problems instead of just reading a problem, then thinking about how you can do it. . . . We work on trying to do a number of different types of problems that may have patterns in them so kids know what they're supposed to be looking for—how to use a table, how to use and make a chart, how to make a good graph. . . . Those are big changes, big changes.

Faith Johnson: "Or getting them to work in groups, to work with other people. To get along, to work in a cooperative group with other people to solve a problem. Someone might have more than one to solve it. . . . Your way may be right, but there may be another approach. . . . The portfolios lend . . . [themselves] to a lot of cooperative groups."

Although both teachers are enthusiastic about the use of portfolios in the classroom, they are less so about their use as part of a statewide assessment. One concern is about the representativeness of the three or four children from their classes whose portfolios are selected for the state-sponsored assessment. A related concern is that although the scores on the best pieces may reflect a child's skills at the end of the school year, they do not reflect the progress made over the year.

Portfolio assessment has the potential to affect not only how teachers work but also how students work. Marge Petit, a middle-school teacher who emerged as a leader of the mathematics assessment committee, put it this way: "Kids became accountable. . . . What I immediately saw in my classroom is that kids in the past who didn't come for extra help suddenly were showing up at my door and saying, you know, I really didn't get that problem, I really don't understand what I was supposed to do there. . . . One of the most important benefits I can think of the whole project . . . has been kids' developing perseverance, stick-to-it-iveness."

Parents have also had to adjust to the implications of portfolio assessment. According to Brian DuPrat: "Initially parents have some concern, some anticipation that we're throwing the times tables out the window, or that they're not going to be learning their fractions, or what about long-division the good old-fashioned way with paper and pencil? And we do our best to allay those fears and assure them . . . what we're teaching is real-life mathematics, and your children are going to be learning fraction skills and the multiplication facts. . . . that is part of our curriculum. Once we get over that hurdle, most parents love the idea."

Faith Johnson found that the emphasis on developing communication skills in the new assessment system has led to questions from some parents: If their child's really good in math and . . . a very good problem solver but not a good communicator, they wonder why I'm pushing so hard for the child to write down what they did and how they solved [the problem]. . . . 'Why does he have to write to you and tell you how he did it? He just did it.'"

Parental concerns are legitimate. Portfolios can measure problem-solving skills, but they can measure other things as well, not all of them useful. Without Vermont's attention to the math curriculum, the portfolios might have become another educational fad that left students no better prepared for the job market.

Doug Harris's efforts to communicate the value of portfolio assessment to the business community have paid off handsomely:

> They want to make sure the kids come to them with marketable skills, and when they talk about marketable skills they talk about . . . self-confidence, to be able to communicate, . . . to express themselves in writing, . . . [and] problem-solving. . . . The portfolios have . . . elicited a lot of interest because the business community says, yeah, these are the kind of things we care about. . . . I can remember . . . doing a portfolio presentation with some of the teachers and the [school] board chair, who's a very successful dairy farmer, [he was] pounding the table and saying, this is exactly what we need.

Although not all superintendents, principals, and teachers in Vermont have embraced the new assessment system as avidly as most in Franklin Northwest have, surveys of teachers and principals indicate that the portfolio assessment is having an impact on instruction. Teachers report devoting substantially more attention to problem solving and communication in teaching mathematics as a result of the program. They also report that students spend more time working in small groups.[12]

In her job as coordinator of the mathematics portfolio network, Jill Rosenblum spends a lot of time talking with teachers and observing how they teach:

> We haven't had what I would call a transformation, but I think that almost every classroom where portfolios have been implemented has seen some change in instruction, and that almost every teacher who's taken any step towards this kind of assessment has changed something about their instruction. . . . They have, at least incrementally, started to change, and to try different things, and to think of them-

selves in a different role. It's a big change we're asking of these people, particularly in math. It's not something they're comfortable with or used to. It's so different from the way they were taught and the way they were trained.[13]

THE FUTURE OF PORTFOLIO ASSESSMENT IN VERMONT

Innovations that change how the work of an organization is carried out are never easy to introduce. NML learned this during the 1980s when it changed the job designs of customer service representatives to introduce one-stop shopping. Vermont continues to learn this today as it grapples with issues raised by the introduction of portfolio assessment. These issues are relevant not only to Vermont; they must be faced by every state attempting to develop high standards for student work and to measure progress toward these standards.

A Critical Tension

Tension persists between the goals of improving instruction and providing reliable data about student performance. Since many teachers value portfolio assessment in classroom instruction but are wary of its use as an accountability system, why not scrap the latter goal and use portfolios solely as a tool for improving instruction? There are three related reasons why pursuit of both goals may be needed, despite the scoring problems. First, taxpayers and employers increasingly want schools to be accountable. It would be much more difficult to retain funding for the network training that teachers find critical to their efforts to incorporate portfolios in their teaching if portfolios were not a central component of an accountability system. Second, the plan to eventually make public school-district-specific scores creates incentives for teachers to learn to use portfolios in their teaching. In other words, the accountability goal may be critical to making progress toward the instructional goal. Finally, if portfolios are not used for accountability purposes, there will be pressure to develop other measures of student skills, such as standardized tests, that will be so used. This will create enormous pressure to abandon portfolio development and to concentrate instruction on helping students to do well on the new instruments. As the adage goes, "What you test is what you get."

Portfolio Assessment in High Schools

From the beginning of his thinking about developing an accountability system in Vermont, Rick Mills knew that the high school must ultimately be part of the plan. Much less clear is the design of a good high school assessment. Differences in the academic programs that high school students take create questions about the best timing of an assessment, and who should be included in the population that is sampled. As Marge Petit described the sampling question: "Do we dip in after kids have finished two years of mathematics? Do we dip in after every kid has finished geometry? What if kids never take geometry?" How these questions are answered could have a major impact on the assessment results.

Perhaps sobered by the challenges of implementing the assessment systems for grades four and eight, the Department of Education has tackled the design of a high school assessment as a long-term research project. Ray Henderson, a high school mathematics teacher in Franklin Northwest Supervisory Union, and Marge Petit head a small group conducting a pilot study in 17 high schools of alternative strategies for assessing the mathematics skills of tenth-graders. The plan is to learn from the pilot which choices about the design of the assessment have marked impacts on the results.

What will the portfolios of high school students look like? As Doug Harris envisions the system: "I would like every kid to walk out of here with a portfolio that represents that kid as a communicator, represents him as a problem solver, represents him as a socially responsible person. . . . [Even though] we're a resource-poor district, I'd love them to be able to [have] an electronic portfolio. . . . Part of it could be video, part of it might be sound. . . . Let's say that you had a kid who . . . wanted to work for a manufacturer. He might be able to really go out and show a videotape of something that he did in a manufacturing setting in school."

Will employers of high school graduates take the time to examine the rich information available in the type of portfolio Doug Harris envisions? Rick Mills realized that this is an issue and enlisted the support of the Vermont Business Roundtable to make the case to employers. To date, more than 200 Vermont employers have joined the "Performance Counts" initiative, under which they commit themselves to use student portfolios, when available, in making hiring decisions. If Vermont employers honor this commitment, it will be a marked departure from current practice in the United States and could markedly increase high school students' incentives to do the hard work needed to master the New Basic Skills.

MEANS AND ENDS

More than in firms like Honda and NML, schools are places where means displace ends. Policies like school-based management and school choice are debated as ends in themselves. They are not connected to the goal that students should learn more rigorous skills. Through the late 1970s, when most high school graduates could get good jobs, the unwillingness to evaluate means was not critical. In today's economy, students who expect good wages need the New Basic Skills, and schools need to choose policies that advance that goal. But evaluating policies meaningfully requires good information on students' mastery of the New Basic Skills. This is the logic behind the Fourth Principle.

Vermont's experience with portfolios illustrates that the principle is not easy to implement. Yet progress continues to be made. In 1994 Vermont's writing assessment was moved from the fourth to the fifth grade to reduce the burden on fourth-grade teachers and to involve teachers at another grade level. The system will continue to change as Rick Mills and his colleagues search for better ways to balance the twin goals of improving teaching and learning and providing reliable information about student performance.

The peculiarities of Vermont demographics—the small size of the state and the relatively high degree of homogeneity of its residents—undoubtedly influenced the strategy of implementing the Fourth Principle. For this reason, Vermont does not provide an exact blueprint for other states' efforts to monitor student progress. But Vermont's experience does provide all states with important lessons.

The first is the importance of developing an assessment strategy that promotes the goal of providing all students with the New Basic Skills—thereby avoiding the Russian nail situation where the measure of performance was not tightly linked with the real goal. Teachers like JoAnne Campbell and Faith Johnson embrace the changes in their teaching practices that portfolio assessment has encouraged because they believe the changes have improved their teaching.

The second lesson is the importance of linking efforts to develop new ways of measuring student skills (the Fourth Principle) with changes designed to improve teaching practices, such as professional development, job redesign, and appropriate incentives (the Second and Third Principles). The state-sponsored network training and summer institutes provide teachers with many opportunities to learn to teach with portfolios. The Franklin Northwest contract provides incentives for teachers to participate in professional development programs. Contracts in other supervisory unions allow teachers several days away from classroom duties to write extensive comments to parents about students' portfolio work and to meet with students and parents to discuss portfolios.

Finally, the Vermont experience demonstrates vividly that developing and implementing a new method of measuring student skills is a long process, that mistakes are inevitable, and that progress comes only with perseverance (the Fifth Principle).

Media stories about portfolio assessment in Vermont typically focus on the new ways of measuring student skills and often neglect the professional development, incentives for teachers, and job redesigns that have been a part of the change effort. This is unfortunate in that constructive change in Vermont has come about because the state's educators embraced the logic that the Five Principles are interdependent and need to be embraced as a package.

CHAPTER 8

THE FIFTH PRINCIPLE
PERSEVERE AND LEARN FROM MISTAKES; THERE ARE NO MAGIC BULLETS

THE SEARCH FOR MAGIC BULLETS

A school, like an automobile plant or insurance company, is a place of individual agendas and vested interests. Change is hard and people yearn for ideas that can make change easy. The yearning for simple solutions is human nature. It is also very dangerous.

The Lesson of Hamtramck

In the early 1980s, General Motors Corporation knew it had problems. The automobile market was becoming increasingly competitive, and General Motors was hamstrung. Much of its labor force worked with dated equipment and had only minimal skills. The workers were further limited by the web of rules written into union contracts. At the new Diamond-Star Motors, production workers were assigned to one of two broad job classifications; many General Motors plants had more than 75 job classifications, each with strictly defined duties. As one industry veteran commented, "When you sneeze and drop a Kleenex, it's a custodian's job to pick it up, not yours."

Confronting these problems was like confronting the Gordian Knot: renegotiating work rules, upgrading training, reorganizing management, unraveling a history of weak productivity.

But if bureaucracy and work rules were GM's weakness, money was its strength. So GM evolved a strategy to spend its way through problems by investing in robotics. Robots—robots that Ford and Chrysler could not afford—would be the sword to sever the knot. Problems in specific areas would not be solved; they would simply be bypassed by computerized machines.

The showcase for these ideas was to be GM's Hamtramck plant, a newly built Cadillac plant outside Detroit.[1] At Hamtramck, 260 robots would handle assembly, welding, and painting operations. Parts would be moved from place to place by 50 automatic vehicles. Laser beams and cameras would be used to monitor quality. Since the point of equipment was to bypass organizational problems, most of those problems were not addressed. Frontline workers received minimal new training. Management structures were left unchanged. Production plans were based on the expectation that the new equipment would work right the first time.

Hamtramck was a disaster. Robots failed to install parts or apply paints properly. Occasionally they destroyed the car on which they were working. Because expectations had been so high, backup systems were weak. Getting the right people to fix robots often required several hours, during which the assembly line was idle. Employees were both frustrated and scared. The cars themselves were awful. Hamtramck was giving the rest of the world lessons in what not to do.

GM believed that the easy job of spending money could

substitute for the messy job of reorganizing work. This is the lesson of Hamtramck: *In any organization, a major obstacle to constructive change is the search for magic bullets—the new technology or set of rules that will painlessly solve problems. While people search for magic bullets, they lack the interest and will to pursue real solutions.*

Hamtramck and the Schools

The lesson of Hamtramck could be drawn from many schools. In schools, the search for magic bullets goes on both inside and outside the building walls. Inside schools, administrators search for actions that will have immediate effects: mandating that all homeroom teachers conduct with their students a three-step program in conflict resolution, moving the English teacher's classroom next to the history teacher's class to promote interdisciplinary teaching, announcing early-morning openhouses to attract parents to the school. No setbacks. No need to regroup or to redesign.

Hoping for an immediate fix is human nature. The danger comes when the hope becomes a manager's test: If an idea doesn't work the first time, it must be a bad idea. By that test, Joe Higgs would have stopped organizing parents when his efforts failed at Blackshear Elementary. Rose Campion, the Cabot superintendent, would have given up on hands-on science for elementary school children when she heard the reactions to the first, disastrous physics course. But Higgs and Campion did not give up. They had sound strategies, they persevered and learned from mistakes, and ultimately they succeeded.

Outside school walls, public officials search for the brilliant idea that will transform all education with a stroke of the pen. The current national debate over U.S. education centers on such ideas:

- More money for schools
- School choice
- School-based management and charter schools
- Statewide academic standards

As advocates portray them, each of these ideas is a magic bullet that will lead automatically to higher student skills.

The Fifth Principle asserts that there are no magic bullets. If we expect schools to teach the New Basic skills to all students, there is no way to avoid the hard work embodied in the Five Principles: getting agreement on the problem, restructuring jobs and incentives, providing frontline workers with training, and developing measures of progress, all backed with perseverance.

Who is right here? If the Five Principles are essential, does it follow that more money or charter schools are useless? Conversely, if school choice or state standards are important, are the Five Principles useless?

We can get to the answer by returning to Hamtramck.

STIMULI FOR CHANGE

GM's Hamtramck robots were a big gamble by a conservative organization. GM made the gamble because it felt enormous market pressure to do something different. Its car sales were declining. Its cost per car was higher than Ford's or Chrysler's costs and much higher than Toyota's. But while the market could tell GM it had to change, it could not tell

GM *how* to change. The gamble on the robots came from GM's internal analysis. Change at Hamtramck, then, was a two-step process. First the market stimulated GM to undertake some kind of change. Then GM designed specific changes which, in the case of Hamtramck, were disastrous.

The national school reform debate is really about that first step—stimulating schools to change. Advocates of more money say it is a lack of funds that prevents schools from changing. Advocates of school choice argue that if parents can withdraw children from a weak school, the school, like GM, will be forced to change. Supporters of school-based management and charter schools argue that giving autonomy to individual schools will unleash them to develop innovative curricula. Advocates of statewide academic standards say that if many of a school's students fail the standards, parents will see the result and will demand change.

Each of these arguments is plausible. The problem arises when advocates make a bigger claim: that a proposal will stimulate not just some kind of change, but the changes that will educate students for tomorrow's jobs. That is a big leap, a leap we can see by considering each of the reform ideas in light of the stories in the previous chapters and other recent experience.

MORE MONEY FOR SCHOOLS?

Will more money for U.S. schools raise student achievement? An answer begins back in Austin, Texas. The $300,000 in extra funds that Zavala received each year as a Priority School was important in improving the school's ability to teach the New Basic Skills to all children. The money helped pay for the school-based health services that contributed to improved student attendance. It helped pay for the Young Scientists program, which gave Zavala students access to the junior high school magnet science program for the first time. The money paid for the professional development and smaller classes that changed the nature of teaching and learning.

But recall that when the Austin School Board designated Zavala a Priority School in 1987, it gave the same designation to 15 other low-income schools. Each of these schools received an extra $300,000 annually. In Zavala and a second school, Ortega, test scores rose, and attendance improved. In the other 14 schools, both low achievement and attendance remained unchanged. Why did two schools do so well while 14 other schools did nothing? The answer lies in how the money was spent. At Zavala and Ortega the money was used to develop and sustain a strategy for changing the daily experiences of students and their teachers. At the 14 other schools, the money was spent primarily on hiring extra teachers to reduce class size; little was done to change what happened inside those classes.

Move to Cabot, Massachusetts, where a generous school budget helped to fund a new elementary science curriculum. Money provided by the Cabot Public Schools Foundation, a parent-run organization, paid for the fifth-grade teachers' course on the physics of light. Money did not make that course a success—the teachers did not learn how to run hands-on physics experiments. But money made it possible to hire David Parnes, the consultant who worked individually with teachers to help them develop the skills the physics course had omitted. In all, money acted like a safety net, allowing the Cabot district to try new things, to make mistakes, and then to recoup. The story ended happily because through the ups and downs, the district focused on using the money to help teachers change how they taught.

Money was important in Boston ProTech and in Vermont. Without funds from the Boston Private Industry Council, there would have been no school counselors like Phillisa Prescott to recruit apprentices and to help them adjust to their hospital jobs. In Vermont, the schools needed extra money from the state legislature to devise the portfolio assessment system and to run the summer workshops and network training that changed how teachers teach mathematics.

In most of these cases, money was important because it funded good ideas: ideas that were clearly linked to raising student skills, ideas that focused on changing how teachers taught and students learned. But if there is no good idea, simply spending money will not produce one. GM Hamtramck and 14 of the 16 Austin priority schools make that point clear.

More money, then, is no guarantee that students will learn the New Basic Skills. In the language of logicians, more money may be *necessary* for improvement but it is never *sufficient* for improvement.

SCHOOL CHOICE AND VOUCHERS

Some advocates of school choice are convinced that "choice *is* a panacea."[2] Even those with less enthusiasm argue that if schools had to compete for students, they would be forced to provide what parents want. And because parents want their children to achieve, the market will force schools to place greater emphasis on raising student skills.

The argument contains an important assumption: that

parents find their children's current achievement wanting. Attitudes are beginning to move in this direction, but they have a long way to go. Recall these facts:

- In the September 1995 Gallup poll, 65 percent of parents gave their oldest child's school a grade of A or B, a level of satisfaction that is only slowly declining (Chapter 1).[3]
- In 1992 almost half of the nation's 17-year-olds could not compute with fractions, decimals, and percentages, recognize geometric figures, and solve simple equations (Chapter 2).
- In 1992 more than half of the nation's 17-year-olds did not read well enough to find, understand, summarize, and explain relatively complicated information, and almost two-thirds could not respond to queries by writing complete statements that contain sufficient information (Chapter 2).[4]

The story of T. A. Vasquez and the Zavala parents shows how parental satisfaction falls quickly when parents understand that their children are poorly educated. But that understanding is not easy to come by. When parents visit a school, certain things stand out—the safety, the discipline, the teacher enthusiasm, the size of the classes. The school's ability to prepare students for the job market is much harder to judge. In this kind of market, it is easy to picture how choice can lead to safer and more pleasant schools—no small accomplishment. It is harder to picture how choice automatically raises student skills.

The picture is confirmed by an experiment now underway in Milwaukee. In the spring of 1990 the Wisconsin legislature enacted the Milwaukee Parental Choice Program, a voucher program aimed at low-income children in the Milwaukee public schools. The program is restricted to children in families with incomes less than 1.75 times the poverty line (about $20,000 for a family of four). The students can use the state payment, $2,987 in 1993–94, to attend private, nonreligious schools. The private schools accept the state payment in lieu of tuition.[5]

Has the program worked? The Wisconsin State Department of Public Instruction commissioned an evaluation team headed by John Witte, a University of Wisconsin political scientist. Supporters of school choice have criticized the evaluation, calling Witte a "hired gun" whose mission is to discredit the program.[6] Despite the vitriol, Witte and his critics agree on four main results:

- The participating children tend to be children who were not doing well in the Milwaukee public schools.
- Parents of participating children are more satisfied with their children's private schools than they were with the Milwaukee public schools their children had attended.
- The participating private schools have lower average per-pupil expenditures than the Milwaukee public schools do.
- Children in the choice program do not have higher reading and mathematics achievement than low-income students attending the Milwaukee public schools.[7]

For those with an open mind, these are important findings. The evaluation shows that choice in Milwaukee has given options to students not doing well in public schools, not just to high-achieving students who want to flee the system. Equally important, the plan has increased parental satisfaction with their children's schools. But to this point, the plan shows no sign of raising student skills.

As always, there are caveats. Catholic schools, traditionally strong in educating low-income students, cannot participate.[8] The private schools that do participate work with less money per student than the Milwaukee public schools. The Milwaukee plan has only been operating for four years.[9] Nevertheless, the results are consistent with our expectation: choice (or any other broad reform) can complement a detailed program to raise student skills, but it is no magic bullet. There is no avoiding the dirty work embodied in the Five Principles.

One more caveat: the Milwaukee plan benefitted low-income students because the Wisconsin legislature designed it that way. But other choice plans distribute benefits in other ways. California's Proposition 174, a 1993 ballot initiative, was a case in point.

Jack Coons is a silver-haired Berkeley law professor with a 30-year passion for improving the education of low-income children. Coons led the 1960s challenge against tying public school funding to local property taxes. Fifteen years later, he concluded that school finance reform had not done much for poor children's achievement. The way to make schools responsive to low-income parents, Coons decided, was to move to a system of vouchers and school choice.

In 1991 Jack Coons and his longtime collaborator, Berkeley law professor Stephen Sugarman, initiated a petition drive to get school vouchers on the California ballot. They designed a plan for all California students which included protections for low-income children. But to get the needed signatures, they had to bargain with groups that had other priorities. As the petition deadline neared, Coons and Sugarman found that they no longer had control of their coalition. Groups who wanted school choice without protections for the poor rewrote the plan. Table 8.1 compares provisions of the original Coons-Sugarman plan and Proposition 174, the voucher initiative that appeared on the California ballot in November 1993.

In the Coons-Sugarman plan, a participating school had to select a certain fraction of its students by lottery and the $5,000 state voucher had to be accepted in lieu of tuition. Together, these requirements meant that low-income students would have expanded options. The revised plan dropped both conditions: a school could select whichever students it chose and it could impose additional tuition on top of the state voucher. What began as a universal choice plan with protections for the poor became a program directed at the well-to-do.[10]

Coons and Sugarman, angered by the changes, withdrew their support. In their view, no choice was better than a choice plan that didn't help the poor. They were relieved when Proposition 174 was defeated. They have since regrouped and continue to advocate a voucher plan aimed at improving education for poor children. Now, as before, the level of support for such plans is unclear.

This evidence makes a simple point: school choice, like more money, is no panacea. To begin with, the impact of any choice plan—including who wins and who loses—is determined by its details. Talking about "choice" in broad terms is not useful.[11] But even a fair choice plan, by itself, has limited power to boost student achievement. A fair choice plan will stimulate school change. But as in all market systems, the nature of change will be driven in large part by schools' attempts to satisfy consumers. Families that

Table 8.1

Characteristics of California Voucher Plans

Issue	Coons-Sugarman Plan	Proposition 174
Dollar amount of voucher	Approximately $5,000	Approximately $2,600
Rules concerning admission of low-income children	School accepting vouchers must reserve 20% of places	No requirement to admit low-income children; school may exclude children on basis of income, gender, disability, or religion
Price school may charge	No more than a family's ability to pay; low-income children may not be charged any fees above value of voucher	No restrictions
Availability of publicly provided transportation for low-income students	Value of voucher adjusted to cover transportation costs for low-income children	No public payment of transportation costs for low-income children
Number of years low-income children can use voucher system before other families participate	Four	Zero
Increase in dollar amount of voucher for disabled children	Dollar amount of voucher adjusted to reflect extra cost of educating disabled child	No adjustment in dollar amount

value skills will seek out schools that have organized around teaching of skills—schools that embrace the Five Principles. Families that are satisfied with their children's skills will seek out other kinds of schools, and achievement levels will not rise. Choice by itself is only part of a solution to the nation's school problem.

CHARTER SCHOOLS AND SCHOOL-BASED MANAGEMENT

Will charter schools or school-based management increase student skills?

In many of the stories we have told, individual initiative has had to fight through centralized authority. Al Melton and Zavala's teachers and parents won most of their fights with the Austin school board. They were ultimately able to provide the health services they wanted, to pay Zavala teachers for time spent in professional development, to use reading texts that the Austin School board had designated for gifted and talented students. But the battles were time-consuming and draining.

Advocates of school-based management argue that these battles are unnecessary. In their view, schools would be more effective if program decisions and resource allocations were made by the adults involved in a given school—principals, teachers, and parents. School boards would hold schools accountable, not by checking compliance with rules, but by monitoring student achievement levels.

On paper, there are many experiments which test these ideas. In reality, the ideas have rarely been tried. One-fourth of the nation's public schools nominally instituted some form of school-based management during the 1980s. But in the vast majority of cases the central office retained control of crucial decisions.[12] In many cases, decision-making authority was also constrained by bargaining agreements. The result was many "nonevents," and it is not surprising that most attempts at "school-based management" have not led to improved student achievement.[13]

But even in a proper experiment, a move to school-based management would only begin the process. A school that wanted to raise student skills would still have to begin by getting agreement that this was the paramount goal—important enough for parents to back up increased demands for homework. It would have to seriously investigate a new curriculum, find strategies for providing teachers with the skills to teach that curriculum, and find ways to measure student progress—in short, the work embodied in the Five Principles. Under school-based management the school would have more freedom to undertake this work. But the school could use its freedom to go in quite different directions.

In the years just ahead, we will learn more about decentralized management from the new wave of charter schools. By 1995, a dozen states had enacted charter school legislation which permits groups of teachers, community agencies, or profit-seeking firms to contract with a school board to operate one or more schools.[14] Charter schools are a promising innovation because they may actually provide the autonomy missing from many school-based management programs. This makes it easier for the school's faculty and parents to agree on a small set of goals including, if they choose, that all students should master the New Basic Skills. Because they stand as distinct entities, charter schools may also have more staying power than a typical school-based management program in which authority is constantly renegotiated.

Will charter schools increase mastery of the New Basic Skills among the nation's students? The concept is too new to have a track record, but observers should keep their eyes on how individual charter schools answer four questions.

- Does the charter school commit itself to a goal like mastery of the New Basic Skills for all its students, or will it emphasize other goals?
- Does the charter school commit itself to serve a fair share of the most difficult-to-educate children and does it have a strategy for attracting such children, or will it discourage applications from such children?
- Does the charter school's contract with the school district provide enough time and enough financial support for the school to persevere and learn from the mistakes that are inevitable in any ambitious new venture?
- Does the charter school commit itself to providing information about student achievement that will allow parents to make sound judgments about the quality of education their children are receiving?

Individual charter schools will answer these questions differently. Those that do commit themselves to providing all students with the New Basic Skills can be a positive force for improving American education, but they will still need the Five Principles to live up to their commitments.

STATEWIDE PERFORMANCE STANDARDS

Will statewide standards raise student skills?

Here, as with the other reforms, the theory is compelling. Recall the evening when Al Melton, the Zavala principal, asked Albert Soto to stand up in front of the PTA meeting and read the Zavala's achievement test scores. When Soto realized how bad the scores were, he became enraged and ultimately withdrew his children from the school. If Soto and the other parents had seen these scores regularly, the theory argues, they would have already known Zavala's problems and would have been working with Melton and Zavala's teachers to improve the school.

Like arguments for school choice, this argument for statewide standards rests on important assumptions. The first is that people can agree on a standard's content. The second is that strategies can be developed to assess whether students have met the standards.

Rick Mills's experience in Vermont shows that both assumptions can be correct—in the long run. But only if the state is willing to undertake a serious marketing effort. For more than a year Mills traveled through the state making the case to parents, teachers, and business groups for both specific educational goals and methods of measuring progress toward those goals. Mills put his time into building the constituency. He left the specifics to committees composed of some of the state's best teachers. The teachers were the ones who specified the emphasis on communication and problem-solving skills and the design of the portfolios.

The Vermont effort drew on the decade-long effort of the National Council of Teachers of Mathematics (NCTM) to determine the mathematics that U.S. students should learn in each grade. Because the NCTM effort was widely praised and proved useful to many states, the federal government supported the National Geographic Society and other professional groups to design standards in other areas: geography, English, and history. These standards, too, were to be held out as models for the states to consider in their own efforts. In practice, these other standards—especially history—have proven far more controversial than mathematics. And when discussion moves from subject content to issues of measurement, the controversy is likely to increase.

Standards are necessary to guide curriculum development and teacher preparation. However, standards will contribute to better education only if they have widespread support, and only if they facilitate rather than impede school-based reform efforts. Only standards that make sense to teachers and parents in affluent Cabot, Massachusetts, in rural Swanton, Vermont, and at Zavala Elementary School in East Austin, Texas, will promote better education for American children. Such standards are likely to be brief, with an emphasis on skills to be learned, rather than lengthy and detailed.

Where standards can be established, there is the question of how they should be used. Mills and the Vermont Department of Education chose to use standards quietly. They decided not to specify cutoff scores for adequate performance. They didn't establish rewards for high-scoring districts or sanctions for low-scoring districts. Instead, they publicized information on student scores by school district and left it up to parents, taxpayers, and teachers to interpret the scores and decide whether changes in the schools were needed.

Other states have used standards in a more vigorous fashion. Six states now provide monetary rewards to the teachers in schools that make progress toward student achievement goals. In some cases, states intervene in districts where progress has been inadequate. Occasionally, poor student performances place teachers' and administrators' jobs in jeopardy.[15] All of these mechanisms try to improve the weak incentives facing most teachers to raise student skills.

But as we saw in Chapter 5, most students face incentives to learn those skills that are equally weak. Plans that improve teacher incentives while leaving student incentives untouched are unlikely to succeed.

In those states where people can agree on standards and how to measure them, visible standards can be useful in raising the alarm that schools need to change. This is a significant contribution. But recognizing the need for change is only the first step. Then comes the hard work of improving schools, and this is where the Five Principles come in.

PERSEVERANCE

Hope dies hard. That is both good news and bad news. It is bad news because people continue to search for one sweeping educational reform that will raise student skills to levels the economy requires. We have discussed these reforms in some detail to kill this hope: to emphasize that no reform can affect student skills unless it complements the hard work of reorganizing individual schools with the Five Principles.

The good news is that hope enables parents, teachers, and principals to persevere in these reorganizations through the inevitable obstacles and mistakes. Austin Interfaith's attempt to increase parent involvement at Blackshear Elementary School failed because Joe Higgs made a mistake: he overestimated the Blackshear principal's interest in improving teaching. But Higgs learned from the Blackshear experience and sought out Al Melton, a principal committed to change. In Zavala itself, the path to improvement was rocky. Albert Soto's angry recitation of the achievement scores widened the gulf between the parents and the teachers. But Al Melton and Joe Higgs found ways to get parents and teachers to agree on something—the need for in-school health services. After the first agreement, life got better.

Throughout all of our stories, the role of perseverance shines through: The Boston PIC dealing with first-year hospital job rotations that left the apprentices on the brink of revolt. Rose Campion and Judy Watson finding new ways of helping the Cabot fifth-grade teachers after the disastrous physics course on light. If Vermont faced fewer crises of faith in developing standards, it was because Rick Mills made the case to the state Board of Education, the legislature, and the business community that development would be a decade-long process.

Throughout the 1980s, observers routinely criticized U.S. business for having excessively short time horizons.[16] Firms like Diamond-Star, Honda, and NML do not have this problem. But what about schools? Can parents and teachers and administrators demonstrate the perseverance required to raise student skills?

If most parents believe their children's skills are adequate, the answer is clearly no. Schools have plenty of work without taking on a hard issue about which nobody cares. But if, as we have argued, parental concern about children's skills is beginning to rise, perseverance and improvement become real possibilities.

Once Americans understand the stakes, change can happen. Smoking is a case in point. In 1940 almost 50 percent of Americans 18 years and older smoked. Cigarettes were included in soldiers' ration packs in World War II and people believed that smoking was a harmless way to reduce tension.

The experts knew better. Epidemiologists saw that the incidence of lung cancer, relatively rare before the twentieth century, began to climb rapidly around 1930. Smoking was the obvious cause. But the findings had not entered public consciousness, and through the 1950s the rate of smoking among American adults stayed relatively constant.

All that changed with the 1964 Surgeon General's Report on Smoking. The report clearly stated that smoking was a health hazard warranting remedial action. Now the information was out. In the years that followed, the federal, state, and local governments engaged in a variety of education efforts, and increased regulation. The Federal Trade Commission mandated that all cigarette packages carry a warning that cigarette smoking was hazardous. Later, federal law banned smoking on domestic airline flights of under six hours. Many states and local governments passed laws requiring nonsmoking sections in public places.

These actions provided the public with information and restricted some actions. But progress in reducing smoking could not be mandated by government; it depended on the actions of citizens. Slowly, but steadily Americans responded. In 1993, 25 percent of Americans smoked, roughly half the comparable figure from 50 years earlier. While the problem of smoking is not solved, great progress has been made over the last 30 years.

There are differences between the smoking problem and the problem of inadequate American education. The Surgeon General's report was a highly publicized event that dramatically increased awareness of the consequences of smoking. The events that demonstrate the need for improved education—the falling wages of high school graduates, the greater instability of all jobs—took place over a decade, diffused across the nation. Once Americans recognized the stakes of smoking, the appropriate action was clear—stop smoking. In the case of a changing economy, the connection takes longer to make. Many parents are just beginning to recognize how economic change has increased the demand for skills—not just skills learned in college, but those that can and should be learned in elementary school and high school. The poll results analyzed in Chapter 1 suggest parental attitudes are beginning to change. But the process is a slow one.

These two differences between the smoking case and the schools case suggest it will be more difficult to retain persistence in improving schools than it has been to reduce smoking. But there is a third difference that cuts the other way. Throughout the effort to educate Americans about the dangers of smoking, cigarette manufacturers have conducted a massive advertising campaign to convince Americans that the Surgeon General's report is not relevant to their lives. Few people are saying that falling wages and increased job instability have nothing to do with American education.

Today, many schoolchildren berate their parents for even looking at a cigarette. Their righteousness, unimaginable 30 years ago, has grown out of millions of people individually changing their attitudes in the face of new evidence. Every day, the economy offers new evidence on the problems of U.S. schools. The evidence is often circumstantial. It has taken some time to penetrate. But it appears that parents are beginning to reassess the stakes of allowing U.S. schools to remain as they are. If this reassessment is underway, all kinds of changes are possible.

CHAPTER 9

GETTING FROM
HERE TO THERE

To secure our nation's future, our schools should be places where all children acquire the New Basic Skills. For most schools, becoming such places will require dramatic departures from current practice. In earlier chapters we saw that change does not have to wait for a state or national program of school reform. Indeed, such top-down initiatives won't make a difference unless they capture the interests of parents, teachers, and children in local schools. But how can their interests be engaged?

A SIMPLE TEST FOR PARENTS

As the experiences of T. A. Vasquez and the other Zavala parents show, learning that their children's education is seriously deficient is the crucial first step in improving it. Few parents have Austin Interfaith to interpret test scores. It is often difficult for parents to judge whether a school is preparing their children for the job market—for example, whether a math class is teaching problem-solving and communication skills. But parents can conduct a simple audit that will help them to make an informed judgment.

222

The audit contains a single question: Where are the children who graduated from this school two years ago? Do elementary school children go on to take algebra in middle school, or do they cluster in remedial courses? Do middle school graduates go on to the good high schools and advanced placement courses, or do they remain in remedial courses and ultimately drop out? And how many of a high school's graduates go on to college? How many, at age 20, are unemployed, finding no one who is willing to hire them?

These are outcomes that all parents can understand and that very few schools collect. Typically, parents learn how well a school's graduates fare only after their own child has graduated—too late to help their child and too late for them to care about supporting a change in the school's priorities. By pressuring schools to report this information regularly, parents can determine on their own whether their children's school is providing the New Basic Skills.

What is true for parents applies equally to teachers, administrators, and school board members. The people in these jobs are kept busy responding to the day-to-day crises that obscure larger problems. Yet these are the people who provide a school with continuity—the people who can translate the experience of today's graduates into lessons for today's students. For this, they need the same overview that parents need: What has happened to the school's recent graduates? How many take algebra in middle school? How many take remedial courses? How many middle school graduates go on to the good high schools and advanced placement courses? How many of a high school's graduates go on to college and how many, at age 20, are unemployed, finding no one who is willing to hire them?

In schools where parents are quiescent, conducting this audit and making it public can be like poking a beehive with a sharp stick. But a school that does not answer these questions, and does not share the answers with parents, is turning its back on its duty.

GETTING STARTED

In earlier chapters, we saw that implementing any one of the first four principles was hard enough. Getting Zavala parents organized took over a year. Developing measures of critical mathematical skills in Vermont continues to this day. It makes logical sense that the Five Principles must be used together. But in a world of limited time and energy, how do you start?

The best answer to this problem comes from the writings of political economist Albert O. Hirschman.[1] Writing about strategies for economic development in the 1950s, Hirschman developed a key insight about "getting from here to there." In those years, the prevailing wisdom was that balanced growth was the most effective economic development strategy for a poor country. Balanced growth meant moving on all fronts at once: raising financing for new factories, building roads so the new factories could easily move raw materials and finished products, establishing schools to train labor for the new factories, and so on. The idea of balance—avoiding bottlenecks—sounded wonderful, but it required a herculean coordination effort well beyond the capability of most governments.

Hirschman's advice was to attack the development problem quite differently. Instead of trying to make progress on all fronts simultaneously, start with the initiative that creates the most pressure for other constructive changes. For example, if the government concentrated on raising funds for new factories, the owners of the new factories would create pressures to build the most-needed roads and to develop the most essential training programs.

Hirschman's logic applies equally well to a strategy for school improvement. Vermont's assessment experience is a case in point. By focusing on the development of portfolio assessments, Rick Mills developed constituencies for other critical changes. Teachers became energized to learn to teach with portfolios when they realized that information on the quality of students' portfolios would be made public. Legislators became willing to fund investments in professional development when they learned that these were a part of Mills's response to their demand for information on student skills. The mandate to develop a system for measuring student skills forced Vermont educators to grapple with tough questions about goals, about which skills are critical and how mastery can be measured. In Vermont, responding to the demand for information about student skills led to other changes, and it was the package of changes that produced changes in children's day-to-day school experiences.

Hirschman's logic also appears in the other stories we have told. In Zavala, getting parents to agree on the problem ultimately led to changes in the classroom. In Boston Pro-Tech, changing the incentives for students through apprenticeships led to pressure, albeit slow pressure, for changes in the curriculum.

Like the process of economic development, the first four principles—defining the problem, providing opportunities and proper incentives, training workers, and measuring progress—form a single, coherent reinforcing system. But because these principles are tightly linked, beginning to work on one of the principles is the most effective way to implement all four. This, then, is the way to begin: Start with the principle that is most likely to generate pressure for other needed changes.

WHEN TO PERSEVERE

There remains a tough question about the Fifth Principle—when to persevere on a new initiative, and when to give up or to dramatically change course. The question dogs all management decisions. Even in Cabot, a school district with substantial resources, the move to hands-on science teaching took time and was punctuated with setbacks. Without perseverance, the move would have been abandoned. At the same time, no amount of perseverance could have saved the robotics at GM's Hamtramck plant because the plan of installing robots while neglecting training and incentives for frontline workers was hopelessly flawed.

The side-by-side examples provide the beginning of an answer. Cabot began with a sensible idea, GM did not, and *this is the first test*. Within a school, any plan worthy of long-term support must ultimately embrace all of the first four principles. There must be a focus on getting frontline workers to agree on the problem, on providing them with appropriate training and incentives, on developing measures of progress. While the test sounds simple, it is a test that many programs fail. It is all too common to hear advocates argue for reforms like school-based management or school choice as ends in themselves. Forcing advocates to explain how a reform will improve student achievement is a powerful aid to clear thinking.

Even with a sensible plan, it may be several years before it is known whether or not an innovation has improved student achievement. During this time, many people will ask whether the plan is on course, or whether dramatic midcourse corrections are needed. Cabot's experience illustrates the way to answer this question. Cabot began with a goal that made sense and with a plan to implement all of the Five Principles. But Jim Benson's physics course did not help Cabot fifth-grade teachers move closer to the goal of hands-on science learning for children because it did not focus directly on the challenge teachers faced. Only when David Parnes began to help individual fifth-grade teachers to learn how to use hands-on methods with children did progress begin. *This is the second test:* In the early stages, when implementation has begun but information on student progress is not yet available, ask whether the plan is changing the daily activities of teachers and students. Unless the daily work of teachers and students changes, student achievement cannot improve.[2]

Judged by these criteria, support for change at Zavala was a good investment. The effort led by Al Melton and Austin Interfaith resulted in an improvement strategy based on the Five Principles. It also led within three years to quite dramatic changes in the way teachers and students spent their time together.

By these same criteria, the extra funding provided to 14 of the 16 Austin Priority Schools was not a good investment. The money in those schools resulted in smaller classes, but it did not lead to any changes that embraced the Five Principles. Nor did it lead to changes in the work that teachers and students did together.

As a thought experiment, consider yourself in the position of a parent, a school board member, or a district super-intendent evaluating the promise of a new charter school. The Five Principles say that its prospects depend on the answers to the following questions: Does the school have clearly defined goals? Are there professional development opportunities for teachers closely linked to pursuit of these goals? Do teachers have incentives to participate in serious professional development and to change the way they teach? What incentives do students face to master the curriculum? Is there an agreed-upon strategy for measuring progress in student achievement? How does the classroom work differ from the work in other schools? Providing answers to these questions will take time; but only a school that can provide the answers has a reasonable chance for success.

Parents, school board members, teachers, and administrators should ask these same questions about any proposal for school improvement: a new professional development program, smaller class sizes, schedule changes, or new ways to assess student skills. Only those proposals that embrace the Five Principles—that change the daily work students and teachers do together—can give students the skills they need to thrive in a changing economy.

THE OTHER HALF OF THE FUTURE

Our story began with a picture of an economy in rapid change. Ten minutes with any newspaper is enough to prove the picture accurate. The good jobs—the jobs that pay enough to support a family—continue to become more complex and to require employees with greater levels of skill. And so economic change hits hardest at the least educated. Recall again the statistic in Figure 2.1: the average 30-year-old man with a U.S. high school diploma now earns $20,000 a year. The average 30-year-old woman with a U.S. high school diploma working year-round, full-time now earns $18,000 a year.[3] As long as our education remains unchanged, these trends will not reverse.

But as the newspaper tells you, economic change now affects more than high school graduates. White-collar jobs at General Electric and Citibank can end in a moment. People with more than a high school diploma have to resell themselves four and five times during their career. As long-term commitments fade, strong education and skills become important for these workers too.

Together, these facts make up one-half of the future. They say, as we said in Chapter 1, that people must see themselves as economic free agents, prepared to prove their market worth at any time. It is a world where you go to war every day, and short of being a millionaire, a very good education is your best armor.

The other half of the future is how we respond to these facts. We have seen in these pages that we face enormous challenges. Many of today's schools continue to educate children for an economy that no longer exists, and many of today's parents are just beginning to recognize the problem. Producing task force reports on improving schools is easy. Providing all children with the New Basic Skills will be hard.

Yet a moment's reflection shows that the work pales before the consequences of doing nothing. If we abdicate the challenge that we now face—if we fail to prepare children for the economic upheaval they will face, if we knowingly educate half of the nation's children for jobs that pay $8.00 per hour—we will create a nation in which few of us—even the successful—will want to live.

ENDNOTES

CHAPTER 1
PREPARING TO MEET THE FUTURE

1. "American Business: Back on Top?" *The Economist* (September 16–22, 1995), p. 64ff.

2. Ina V. S., Mullis and others, *Report in Brief: NAEP Trends in Academic Progress* (Washington, D.C.: National Center for Education Statistics), July 1994.

3. Stanley M. Elam and Lowell C. Rose, "The 27th Annual Phi Delta Kappa/Gallup Poll of the Public's Attitudes toward the Public Schools," *Phi Delta Kappan* 77(September 1995)1: 41–56.

4. The issue was further submerged because raising student skills is hard to do—harder than adding a new curriculum unit on the health effects of smoking.

5. Stanley M. Elam and Lowell C. Rose, "The 27th Annual Phi Delta Kappa/Gallup Poll of the Public's Attitudes toward the Public Schools," *Phi Delta Kappan* 77(September 1995)1: 43.

6. Stanley M. Elam and Lowell C. Rose, "The 27th Annual Phi Delta Kappa/Gallup Poll of the Public's Attitudes toward the Public Schools," *Phi Delta Kappan* 77(September 1995)1: 46–47. The wording of the questions in the 1989 and 1991 polls is slightly different.

7. Jean Johnson, *Assignment Incomplete: The Unfinished Business of Education Reform*, Public Agenda, 1995.

8. *Statistical Abstract of the United States 1995*, U.S. Department of Commerce, Bureau of the Census, Washington, D.C., 1995, pp. 121, 123; *Statistical Abstract of the United States 1982–83*, U.S. Department of Commerce, Bureau of the Cen-

sus, Washington, D.C., 1983, p. 107; *Historical Statistics of the United States, Colonial Times to 1970,* Part 1, Chapters A–M (White Plains, N.Y.: Kraus International Publications), p. 175. The earnings figure cited in the text as earnings for 1950 is actually the figure for 1951.

9. David A. Hounshell, *From the American System to Mass Production, 1800–1832* (Baltimore: Johns Hopkins University Press, 1984).

10. David Tyack and Larry Cuban, *Tinkering toward Utopia* (Cambridge, Ma.: Harvard University Press), pp. 29–33.

11. Richard J. Murnane, John B. Willett, and Frank Levy, "The Growing Importance of Cognitive Skills in Wage Determination," *Review of Economics and Statistics* 77(May 1995)2: 251–266.

CHAPTER 2

SKILLS FOR A MIDDLE-CLASS WAGE

1. In October 1991, Chrysler sold its share of the venture to Mitsubishi.

2. The computer-use statistics are based on tabulations of the October 1984 and October 1993 Current Population Surveys compiled by David H. Autor, and reported in his 1995 unpublished paper entitled "Estimating the Impacts of Computerization on Wages, Education Shares, and the Employment of Secretaries and Managers, 1984–1993: A Panel Approach," Harvard University, Cambridge, Ma.

3. The statistics on computer use by high school seniors were computed by the authors from data in the second follow-up of NELS88, the National Educational Longitudinal Study of students who were first surveyed as eighth-graders in 1988.

4. By the term "semistructured problem" we mean a problem in which part of the task is to figure out what types of computations are necessary to solve it.

5. See Ina V. S. Mullis and others, *Report in Brief: NAEP 1992 Trends in Academic Progress* (Washington, D.C.: National Center for Education Statistics), July 1994, pp. 12–13.

6. Too high skill requirements also raise motivational problems. As one Ford executive said, "If you talk to the engineers, they'll tell you that all production line workers should know how to use personal computers and run spreadsheets. What the engineers don't understand is that if I hired production workers who could do those things, they wouldn't be able to stand the job. They'd quit within two weeks."

7. Claudia Goldin and Robert Margo, "The Great Compression: The Wage Structure in the United States at Mid-Century," *Quarterly Journal of Economics* 107(February 1992): 1–34.

8. Daniel E. Hecker, "Reconciling Conflicting Data on Jobs for College Graduates," *Monthly Labor Review* (July 1992), pp. 3–12.

9. Authors' tabulations of data from Current Population Surveys.

10. Philip Moss and Chris Tilly, "'Soft' Skills and Race: An Investigation of Black Men's Employment Problems," Working paper, Department of Policy and Planning, University of Massachusetts at Lowell, May 1995. This same pattern is reported in *Learning a Living: A Blueprint for High Performance*, The Secretary's Commission on Achieving Necessary Skills (SCANS), U.S. Department of Labor, Washington, D.C., April 1992.

11. While the tests were not exactly identical in every item, Educational Testing Service used a model based on item-response theory (IRT) to create scores for the two tests that were comparable. It is these IRT scores that we used in our analysis.

12. We use the terms "mathematical skills" and "cognitive skills" interchangeably in describing our results. The reason is that the patterns are similar when scores on the reading tests are used in place of scores on the mathematics tests.

13. For a detailed discussion of the statistical evidence, see Richard J. Murnane, John B. Willett, and Frank Levy, "The Growing Importance of Cognitive Skills in Wage Determination," *Review of Economics and Statistics* 77(May 1995)2: 251–266. A recent survey of employers also finds evidence that a majority have increased skill requirements for employees in the last three years. See "I. Employer Practices," Results from the EQW National Employer Survey, National Center on the Educational Quality of the Workforce, University of Pennsylvania, Philadelphia, 1995.

14. As Table 1 of the Murnane, Willett, Levy (1995) paper shows, the 20 percent estimate from NLS72 data and HS&B data for the growth in the college wage premium between 1978 and 1986 for 24-year-old women is less than the comparable estimate based on data from the Current Population Surveys.

15. "American Business: Back on Top?" *The Economist* (September 16–22, 1995), p. 64ff.

16. See Katherine S. Newman and Chauncy Lennon, "Finding Work in the Inner City: How Hard Is It Now? How Hard Will It Be for AFDC Recipients?" Working paper, Department of Anthropology, Columbia University, February 1995.

17. In 1980, immigrants accounted for about 11 percent of workers who were high school dropouts. See George Borjas, Richard Freeman, and Lawrence Katz, "Searching for the Effects of Immigration on the Labor Market," *American Economic Review Papers and Proceedings,* 86(May 1996)2.

CHAPTER 3
FIVE PRINCIPLES FOR MANAGING
FRONTLINE WORKERS

1. This paragraph is a summary of material that appeared in an article entitled "Workbench" that appeared in *Pillar,* the

home office magazine of Northwestern Mutual Life, 51(1989)1: 18.

2. Frederick W. Taylor, *The Principles of Scientific Management* (New York: W. W. Norton, first published in 1911), p. 45.

3. Paul Osterman, "How Common Is Workplace Transformation and Who Adopts It?" *Industrial and Labor Relations Review* 47(January 1994)2: 173–188.

4. "The EQW National Employer Survey: First Findings," National Center on the Educational Quality of the Workforce, University of Pennsylvania, Philadelphia, 1995.

5. Edward E. Lawler III, Susan A. Mohrman, and Gerald E. Ledford, Jr., *Creating High Performance Organizations* (San Francisco: Jossey-Bass), 1995.

CHAPTER 4

THE FIRST PRINCIPLE: AGREE ON THE PROBLEM

1. Stanley M. Elam and Lowell C. Rose, "The 27th Annual Gallup/Phi Delta Kappa Poll of the Public's Attitudes toward the Public Schools," *Phi Delta Kappan* 77(September 1995)1: 41–56; and Jean Johnson, *Assignment Incomplete: The Unfinished Business of Education Reform*, Public Agenda, 1995.

2. Harold W. Stevenson and James W. Stigler, *The Learning Gap* (New York: Summit Books, 1992), chapter 5.

3. Jean Johnson, *Assignment Incomplete: The Unfinished Business of Education Reform*, Public Agenda, 1995, p. 33.

4. "The Texas I.A.F. Vision for Public Schools: Community of Learners," Austin, Texas: Texas Interfaith Education Fund, 1990.

5. The description of the Right Question Project is based on interviews with Project staff and the external evaluator, Donna Muncey, supplemented by the description in *Deliver-*

ing on the Promise: Positive Practices for Immigrant Students (Boston: National Coalition of Advocates for Students, 1994), pp. 168–170.

CHAPTER 5
THE SECOND PRINCIPLE: PROVIDE THE RIGHT INCENTIVES AND OPPORTUNITIES

1. The concept of treaties is developed in Arthur G. Powell, Eleanor Farrar, and David Cohen, *The Shopping Mall High School: Winners and Losers in the Educational Marketplace* (Boston: Houghton-Mifflin, 1985).

2. The best high school students in the Boston public schools attend schools with entrance examinations such as Boston Latin School. None of the exam schools participated in Pro-Tech.

3. The legal risk arises when an employer is accused of applying hiring criteria not directly related to a job (*Griggs* v. *Duke Power Co.* (401 U.S. 424 [1971])). When an employer knows he may have to justify why he required applicants to have an "A" in algebra, he may find it easier simply to drop the requirement.

4. Alternatively, employers fill the more serious jobs with older, outside applicants.

5. See *The American Freshman: National Norms,* Washington D.C., American Council on Education and UCLA Graduate School of Education, various editions.

6. By "unexpected" we mean achievement that differs from a predicted level based on the students' family income, parental education, and other contributors to socioeconomic status.

7. Susan Goldberger, "Creating an American-style Youth Apprenticeship Program: A Formative Evaluation of Project ProTech." A report prepared for the Boston Private Industry Council, Boston, Ma., Jobs for the Future, February 1993.

8. For more information on career academies, see David Stern, Marilyn Raby, and Charles Dayton, *Career Academies: Partnerships for Reconstructing American High Schools* (San Francisco: Jossey Bass, 1992).

9. Goldberger, p. 6.

10. Edward Pauly, Hilary Kopp, and Joshua Haimson, *Home-Grown Lessons: Innovative Programs Linking School and Work* (San Francisco: Jossey-Bass, 1995).

11. Edward Pauly and others, *Home-Grown Lessons* (San Francisco: Jossey-Bass, 1995).

CHAPTER 6
THE THIRD PRINCIPLE:
TRAIN THE FRONTLINE WORKERS

1. Susan Loucks-Horsley and others, *Elementary School Science for the '90s* (Andover, Ma.: The Network, 1990).

2. Tracy Kidder, *Among Schoolchildren* (Boston: Houghton-Mifflin, 1989), p. 32.

3. "Goals 2000: Educate America Act," federal legislation signed by President Clinton in March 1994.

4. Two teachers did not complete the course due to child care problems, and a third due to illness.

5. This section draws heavily from the description of the SEED project provided in Mark St. John and others, *Reforming Elementary Science Education in Urban Districts* (Inverness, Ca.: Inverness Research Associates, 1994). The authors also benefitted from conversations with Jennifer Yuré and Jerry Pine, who played key roles in the design of the program.

6. Lynne Miller and David L. Silvernail, "Wells Junior High School: Evolution of a Professional Development School," in L. Darling-Hammond (ed.), *Professional Development Schools,* Teachers College Press, pp. 28–49. This section also

draws on an interview with Susan Walters, the school-based site coordinator for the extended teacher education program at Wells.

7. Miller and Silvernail, pp. 41–42.

8. This description draws from several sources: interviews with Judy Buchanan and Susan L. Lytle, directors of the Philadelphia Writing Project; interviews with several participating teachers; and a paper by Elizabeth Useem, Judy Buchanan, Emily Meyers, and Joanne Matule-Schmidt entitled "Urban Teacher Curriculum Networks and Systematic Change," which was presented at the Annual Meetings of the American Educational Research Association, San Francisco, April 1995. The quotations from participants in the Philadelphia Writing Project are taken from the paper by Useem and others, 1995.

CHAPTER 7

THE FOURTH PRINCIPLE:

MEASURE PROGRESS REGULARLY

1. *Vermont Assessment Program Summary of Assessment Results 1992–93,* Vermont State Department of Education, Montpelier, November 1993.

2. *The Condition of Education in Vermont,* Vermont State Department of Education, Montpelier, 1993.

3. Paul G. LeMahieu, Joanne T. Eresh, and Richard C. Wallace, Jr., "Using Student Portfolios for a Public Accounting," *The School Administrator,* December 1992, pp. 8–15.

4. Linda Darling-Hammond and Jackquiline Ancess, *Authentic Assessment and School Development,* National Center for Restructuring Education, Schools, and Teaching, Teachers College, Columbia University, New York, June 1994, pp. 8–9.

5. National Science Board, *Science and Engineering Indicators,* Washington, D.C., 1987.

6. National Council of Teachers of Mathematics, *Curriculum and Evaluation Standards for School Mathematics,* Washington, D.C., 1989.

7. The description of the mathematics assessment system is taken from Daniel Koretz, Brian Stecher, and Edward Deibert, *The Vermont Portfolio Program: Interim Report on Implementation and Impact, 1991–92 School Year,* Rand Corp., July 31, 1992.

8. *Vermont Mathematics Portfolio Project: Teacher's Guide,* Vermont Department of Education, September 1991.

9. The Vermont Department of Education distributed for comments a sample assessment report entitled "Dewey, Vermont: Assessment Results" (no date).

10. See Daniel Koretz, Daniel McCaffrey, Stephen Klein, Robert Bell, and Brian Stecher, *The Reliability of Scores from the 1992 Vermont Portfolio Assessment Program: Interim Report,* Rand Institute on Education and Training, December 4, 1992.

11. Daniel Koretz, Stephen Klein, Daniel McCaffrey, and Brian Stecher, *Interim Report: The Reliability of Vermont Portfolio Scores in the 1992–93 School Year,* Rand Corp., December 1993, p. 5. When scores were averaged across dimensions, the correlations between readers' mathematics scores were higher: for fourth-grade scores, .60 in 1992 and .72 in 1993; for eighth-grade scores, .53 in 1992 and .79 in 1993.

12. Daniel Koretz, Brian Stecher, Stephen Klein, and Daniel McCaffrey, "The Vermont Portfolio Assessment Program: Findings and Implications," *Educational Measurement: Issues and Practice* 13 (Fall 1994)3:5–16.

13. For an insightful discussion of the difficulties in changing how teachers teach mathematics, see David K. Cohen, "A Revolution in One Classroom: The Case of Mrs. Oublier," *Educational Evaluation and Policy Analysis* 12(Fall 1990)3: 311–329.

CHAPTER 8
THE FIFTH PRINCIPLE: PERSEVERE AND LEARN FROM
MISTAKES; THERE ARE NO MAGIC BULLETS

1. The description of the experience at Hamtramck is based on Maryann Keller, *Rude Awakening: The Rise, Fall and Struggle for Recovery of General Motors* (New York: William Morrow, 1989).

2. John E. Chubb and Terry M. Moe, "Choice *Is* a Panacea," *Brookings Review* 8(Summer 1990)3: 4–12.

3. Stanley M. Elam and Lowell C. Rose, "The 27th Annual Phi Delta Kappa/Gallup Poll of the Public's Attitudes toward the Public Schools, *Phi Delta Kappan* 77(September 1995)1: 41–56.

4. Ina V. S. Mullis et al., *Report in Brief: NAEP 1992 Trends in Academic Progress* (Washington, D.C.: National Center for Education Statistics, 1994), pp. 12–14.

5. John F. Witte, Andrea B. Bailey, and Christopher A. Thorn, "Third-Year Report: Milwaukee Parental Choice Program," Department of Political Science and Robert La Follette Institute of Public Affairs, University of Wisconsin–Madison, December 1993; and John F. Witte, Christopher A. Thorn, Kim M. Pritchard, and Michele Claibourn, "Fourth Year Report: Milwaukee Parental Choice Program," Department of Political Science and Robert La Follette Institute of Public Affairs, University of Wisconsin–Madison, December 1994. As currently operated, the program is limited to 1.5 percent of students in the Milwaukee public schools.

6. Daniel McGroarty, "School Choice Slandered," *The Public Interest* 117(Fall 1994), pp. 94–111.

7. Witte and others (1993), pp. 22–23.

8. Anthony S. Bryk, Valerie E. Lee, and Peter B. Holland, *Catholic Schools and the Common Good* (Cambridge, Ma.: Harvard University Press, 1993).

9. The most recent evaluation of the Milwaukee choice program describes outcomes in the fourth year of the program.

10. The descriptions of the Coons and Sugarman voucher initiative and Proposition 174 come from the following sources: John E. Coons and Stephen D. Sugarman, *Scholarships for Children* (Berkeley, Calif.: Institute of Governmental Studies Press, 1992), and "Education. Vouchers," Initiative Constitutional Amendment, Analysis by the Legislative Analyst, California Ballot Pamphlet, Sacramento, November 1993.

11. For a thoughtful discussion of the conditions under which choice may promote improvements in an organization's performance, see Albert O. Hirschman, *Exit, Voice, and Loyalty* (Cambridge, Ma.: Harvard University Press, 1970).

12. Joan First and others, *The Good Common School* (Boston: National Coalition of Advocates for Students, 1991), pp. 29–31.

13. See Anita A. Summers and Amy W. Johnson, "A Review of the Evidence on the Effects of School-Based Management Plans," paper presented at the *Conference on Improving the Performance of America's Schools: Economic Choices,* National Academy of Sciences, October 12–13, 1994, Washington, D.C.; also Bruce Bimber, *The Decentralization Mirage: Comparing Decisionmaking Arrangements in Four High Schools* (Santa Monica, Calif.: Rand, 1994).

14. Chris Pipho, "Stateline: The Expected and the Unexpected," *Phi Delta Kappan* 76(June 1995)10: 742.

15. Richard F. Elmore, Charles H. Abelmann, and Susan H. Fuhrman, "The New Accountability in State Education Reform: From Process to Performance," paper presented at the Brookings Institution Conference on Performance-Based Approaches to School Reform, Washington, D.C., April 6–7, 1995.

16. Robert H. Hayes and William Abernathy, "Managing Our Way to Decline," *Harvard Business Review* 58 (July/August 1980)4: 67–77.

CHAPTER 9
GETTING FROM HERE TO THERE

1. Albert O. Hirschman, *The Strategy of Economic Development* (New Haven, Conn.: Yale University Press, 1958).

2. For a rich description of this perspective, see Edward Pauly, *The Classroom Crucible: What Really Works, What Doesn't, and Why* (New York: Basic Books, 1991).

3. The annual earnings figures for 30-year-old males and females reported in the text are not comparable because the figure for males is based on all 25- to 34-year-old male high school graduates with positive earnings, while the figure for females is based on 25- to 34-year-old female high school graduates who worked year-round full-time. Male 25- to 34-year-old high school graduates working year-round full-time in 1993 had median earnings of $22,400. Among 25- to 34-year-old female high school graduates with positive earnings (including those who worked less than year-round full-time), median earnings in 1993 were $13,736.

INDEX